Excellence
in
Upper-Level Writing
2016/2017

**The Gayle Morris
Sweetland Center for Writing**

Edited by
Dana Nichols

Published in 2017 by Michigan Publishing
University of Michigan Library

Michigan Publishing
1210 Buhr Building
839 Greene Street
Ann Arbor, MI 48104
lib.pod@umich.edu

ISBN 978-1-60785-417-3

Table of Contents
Excellence in Upper-Level Writing

Excellence in Upper-Level Writing 2016/2017

Sweetland Writing Prize Chair

Dana Nichols

Sweetland Writing Prize Committee

Samer Ali

Alena Aniskiewicz

Gary Beckman

Anne Gere

Elizabeth Goodenough

Christian Greenhill

Jacqueline Larios

Shuwen Li

Vilma Mesa

Sheila Murphy

Lori Smithey

Elizabeth Tinsley Johnson

Administrative Support

Laura Schulyer

Aaron Valdez

Winners List

Granader Family Prize for Excellence in Upper-Level Writing (Sciences)

Natalie Andrasko "Refugees struggle rejoining medical field after resettlement"
Nominated by Emilia Askari, Environ 320

Hadley Tuthill "Uncovering Food Insecurity Among College Students,
a Tricky Population"
Nominated by Julie Halpert, Environ 320

Granader Family Prize for Excellence in Upper-Level Writing (Social Sciences)

Meredith Fox "Would You Know It If You Saw It?: Gender Differences in
College Students' Ability to Identify Sexual Assault"
Nominated by Kimberly Hess, Sociology 310

Michael Gawlik "Chapter 1: The Characters"
Nominated by John Carson, History 499

Granader Family Prize for Excellence in Upper-Level Writing (Humanities)

Courtney Cook "10 Months In Europe"
Nominated by Jaimien Delp, English 325 / Art of the Essay

Claire Wood "On Nights Like These"
Nominated by John Rubadeau, English 425 / Advanced Essay Writing

Nominees List

Student Name	Instructor Name
Natalie Andrasko	Emilia Askari
Zachary Arrington	Mary Pena
Caitlin Boland	Jeannie Hahl
Heather Buja	Maria Lasonen-Aarnio
Courtney Cook	Jaimien Delp
Madeleine Fougere	Omolade Adunbi & Amanda Kaminski (GSI)
Meredith Fox	Kimberly Hess
Genevieve Friedman	Emilia Askari
Michael Gawlik	John Carson
William Hammond	Jennifer Metsker
Allison Lang	Kimberly Hess
Kallan Larsen	Jeannie Hahl
Lauren Lukens	Julie Halpert
Qianya Meng	Jaimien Delp
Dylan Nelson	John Carson
Reena Pang	Omolade Adunbi & Amanda Kaminski (GSI)
Aaron Pelo	Linda Gregerson
Lia Salmansohn	Mary Pena
Olivia Statman	Mark Mizruchi
Hadley Tuthill	Julie Halpert
Christophern Vanetten	Maria Lasonen-Aarnio
Claire Wood	John Rubadeau

Introduction

The book you hold in your hands contains evidence, important evidence about what college students are able to accomplish as writers. Each of the students represented here was enrolled in an Upper Level Writing Requirement (ULWR) course, which every student in the College of Literature, Science and the Arts is required to complete in order to graduate. Many students take ULWR courses in their majors so they can learn to write effectively in that field, but many others complete the ULWR in a field outside the major because writing in another area gives them, they say, a wider, more interdisciplinary, perspective.

The writing included here was identified by instructors as exceptional, and the introductions, written by the nominating faculty member, explain the features that make it worthy of a prize. These instructors deserve special credit for creating contexts where students could write regularly, receive helpful feedback, and deepen their understanding of ways to make a convincing argument. Looking at the assignments that inspired this writing shows another important contribution made by instructors; they took care in designing prompts for writing that would be both clear and challenging.

Of course our student writers deserve special praise. After producing a draft they took up suggestions from peers and instructors and revised their writing again and again. In so doing, they gave increased attention to addressing their audience, to clarifying what they wanted to accomplish with the writing, and to making their prose both accessible and stylish. As the selections included here show, college student writers can, with the support of programs like the ULWR, produce very effective prose. In a society that continually looks for skilled writers, in business, in the professions, and in a variety of other spaces, it is reassuring to see evidence that our students are ready to take up the challenges of writing for 21st century audiences.

A generous gift from the Granader family provides a cash award for each student writer. This, along with a certificate recognizing their excellence in writing, gives prize-winning students tangible evidence of the importance of writing well. At the same time, these students provide a model and inspiration for their peers. *Excellence in Upper-Level Writing 2017* will join volumes from past years in an online format where it can be used in ULWR instruction and in other courses. Thanks to Dana Nichols for careful editing and Aaron Valdez for a design that creates an appropriately professional context for displaying this writing.

Participants in the Sweetland Seminar—faculty and advanced graduate students committed to integrating writing into their coursea and helping students become better writers—serve as judges for the Granader Family Prize for Excellence in Upper-Level Writing. This year's readers were: Samer Ali, Alena Aniskiewicz, Gary Beckman, Anne Gere, Elizabeth Goodenough, Christian Greenhill, Jacqueline Larios, Shuwen Li, Vilma Mesa, Shelia Murphy, Lori Smithey, and Elizabeth Johnson Tinsley. Thanks to each and all for making the difficult choices involved in selecting the winners of this year's prizes for excellence in upper-level writing.

Anne Ruggles Gere, Director
Sweetland Center for Writing

Winning Essays
Granader Prize for Excellence in Upper-Level Writing (sciences)

Refugees struggle rejoining medical field after resettlement

Natalie Andrasko

From Environ 320
Nominated Emilia Askari

As the co-instructor for Environ 320, a course in environmental and public health journalism, I nominate Natalie Andrasko for the Granader Family Upper-Level Writing Prize. Our class requires each student to report, write and re-write a news feature on a topic of the student's choice related to the environment or public health. While most students gravitate towards campus-centered stories, Natalie was more ambitious. She chose to tackle an international story with little Ann Arbor connection: the plight of Middle Eastern refugees with medical training. Natalie gathered facts for this story with great attention to detail, empathy for her subjects and tenacity. In the run-up to the presidential election, many immigrants became more fearful of trouble with government officials – and more reluctant to speak publicly about their plight. This created a daunting challenge for Natalie. Many students might have given up and tried to switch story topics. Not Natalie. She persisted, eventually landing an interview with a medical professional who is a refugee from the Middle East. He even allowed Natalie to photograph him. Although Natalie is not from Michigan, on her own she found a way to travel more than an hour east of Ann Arbor, to the Detroit suburb where this medical professional works. In her well-organized story, Natalie also shared solid statistics that help readers understand why they should care about medical professionals who are refugees from the Middle East. The resulting story offers a fresh angle on the widely-reported topic of Middle Eastern refugees. It is a story that would be appropriate on the web site of many national news outlets. My teaching partner and I did not identify Natalie as a stand-out from the first couple of weeks of the term. She's a bit quiet. It was Natalie's eagerness to take on a big reporting challenge, her determination and her responsiveness to criticism that ultimately made her news feature so strong. Every student in our class is required to revise the first draft of his or her news feature. Natalie was among the few who took the additional step of submitting an optional interim draft as she continued to polish both her reporting and writing. I am pleased to nominate Natalie's news feature for the Sweetland Prize.

Emilia Askari

Refugees struggle rejoining medical field after resettlement

Kaes Almasraf with his Refugee Health Empowerment Program recertification certificate in ACCESS' Sterling Heights, MI office

Kaes Almasraf remembers exactly how he felt the day he arrived in Michigan three years ago as a refugee. "Just close your eyes and then open your eyes… you're in a new country with new people, new culture, new system, new everything. Why am I here? What am I going to do?" Almasraf, 38, was working as a dentist and manager of a dental clinic for seven years in Baghdad before he gained refugee status and was resettled in Michigan with his wife and then two-year-old daughter. When he arrived in America, he soon discovered he would be forced to start over, beginning the grueling process of re-entering the medical field. Almasraf now works to empower other refugees to achieve their full potential in their medical fields. "They were dentists or they were doctors in their home country—why here, they are nothing?"

Since May 2011, over 13,000 Syrian refugees have been relocated to the US, according to CNSNews.com. More than 1,404 of them have landed in Michigan, the second most popular state for refugee resettlement. The Syrian refugee crisis has captivated the world, as news outlets stream footage of wreckage in cities, violence, and overcrowded refugee camps. President Trump's recent

January 27th executive order banning immigration for over 218 million people from Syria and Iraq, where Almasraf is from, and five other predominantly Muslim nations adds a new very complicated layer of uncertainty to this issue. After the 120-day ban is lifted, Trump has stated that he plans to accept 50,000 people, half as many as Obama's administration, and priority will be given to Christian refugees. Amidst lawsuits, protests from the American Civil Liberties Union, and claims that the ban is unconstitutional, federal judge Ann Donnelly responded by issuing a stay preventing deportations of people detained on entry to the United States. While the world waits for answers as to how this conflict will unfold, for refugees like Almasraf and the 218 million people now banned from entering the United States, the future is uncertain.

According to the U.S. Office of Refugee Resettlement, every refugee 18 or older is issued a work permit and expected to begin steady work within six months of resettlement. This short deadline, combined with the small government-provided stipend of $1,200 given per person upon arrival and the limit of 90 days of assistance resettlement agencies are allowed to provide, puts enormous pressure on refugees to find jobs immediately. In addition, they must enroll their children in schools, find housing, and learn English. For refugees who were medical professionals in their home countries, this restrictive and confusing process leads many to settle for low-paying jobs outside their field of expertise.

"A lot of them end up not working in the health care field, so they end up taking jobs unfortunately at fast food restaurant chains or in factories, so a lot of the skills they worked so hard for go to waste," Kshama Vaghela said. Vaghela is the Public Health Coordinator at the Office of Refugee Resettlement-funded Arab Community Center for Economic and Social Services (ACCESS), the largest refugee resettlement organization in Michigan. ACCESS' forty-year presence in Dearborn, which has the largest proportion of Arab Americans in the country and second most Syrian refugees in Michigan, puts them in a unique position to directly impact the refugee community. Vaghela works specifically with medical professional refugees, linking them to internships, college courses, resume workshops, mock interviews, and English language training.

The recertification process is daunting for refugees with medical backgrounds. Their degrees need to be translated into an American equivalent and they must pass the Medical Licensing Examination. Often, they have to retake medical school classes. Every refugee must also pass the Test of English as a Foreign Language exam to establish that their English is satisfactory, but for refugees who don't pass this very challenging exam, getting hired is extremely difficult.

Nicole Feinberg, a case worker at Jewish Family Services, a prominent Washtenaw County nonprofit, has heard many refugees express frustration at repeatedly being denied jobs by employers who don't accept their foreign degrees or claim that English isn't satisfactory. But Feinberg has noticed that some of these jobs, like at grocery stores, don't even require a degree, suggesting an underlying reason why refugees are getting denied employment—stigma. "They feel that they have to go ten steps ahead of an American applicant to prove that they're not a terrorist and they aren't trying to work in your agency to kill you," says Feinberg.

Almasraf believes this xenophobic rhetoric may stem from people simply not understanding Arab culture, mistakenly thinking refugees don't know how to use computers or function in American jobs. This lack of understanding can impact the quality of care medical professionals can provide refugees. If the recertification process can be made more efficient and more refugees are in the medical field, these refugee medical professionals may be able to connect more deeply with patients from their own community, providing higher quality care. "You need to live the situation to understand it," Almasraf says, which is why he chose to work at ACCESS as a case manager after completing the Refugee Health Empowerment Program to give back to the refugee community. The need for more refugees in the medical field will benefit every American, not just refugees, Almasraf adds, because "Everybody needs a dentist, everybody needs a doctor, everybody needs a specialist."

"I like my home. I like my friends, I like my neighbors, my job, my clinic. I miss all these things," reflects Almasraf on the sudden absence of these comforts upon arriving in the United States. "When you are alone, even in paradise, you're going to be lost." Almasraf's dedication to his job guiding other refugees through the recertification process, combined with the efforts from nonprofits across the country, will help lessen this feeling of isolation. Looking back on his move from Iraq to the American Midwest just three years ago, Almasraf is optimistic about the future for his family and other refugees in the medical field, despite the current political climate surrounding refugees. "There were many challenges. But if you need something good for you and your family, you're going to do your best. You're going to stand again, you're going to breathe again, you're going to make decisions—right decisions in order to be good for yourself, good for your family, and good for your new country."

Uncovering Food Insecurity Among College Students, a Tricky Population

Hadley Tuthill

From Environ 320

Nominated Julia Halpert

In her news feature, Hadley Tuthill brought to the public's attention a vulnerable population: college students who struggle to afford food. The article highlighted the dramatic scope of the problem with startling new research showing that 61 percent of low and moderate income college students at Wisconsin universities were food insecure at some point during the school year, with 42 percent of respondents saying that they cut or skipped meals because they did not have adequate funds. Hadley reached out to a variety of leading experts to discuss the factors driving the growth in food insecurity among these students. Particularly alarming was the finding that many students were forced to choose between purchasing textbooks and eating a nutritious meal. She interviewed leading experts from all over the country and included their comments about why this is occurring, as well as the potential consequences of this situation. Moving the story forward in a productive way, Hadley included programs designed to respond to the needs of students facing food insecurity. The vast number of sources included in the piece ensured she provided an extremely comprehensive discussion of this important issue. This article stands out not just for the quality of the information, but in the eloquent way the story was written. Hadley's descriptive writing has a poetic style. The way she describes the opening scene of a campus food bank makes it easy to visualize this scene. This makes for a gripping introduction. The piece is extremely well organized, as Hadley easily shifts from the research to experts' discussion of the ramifications of the situation. The quotes clearly convey the heartbreaking choices that financially challenged students must face. Hadley concludes this piece in a hopeful way, letting the reader know developments that may make a positive difference. Hadley identified an important issue that I have not seen covered in this particular manner with so much depth. Her engaging writing and the high level experts she featured make this piece the caliber of a professional journalism article. I believe that Hadley is a worthy candidate for the Granader Family Upper-Level Writing prize and appreciate you considering her article.

Julia Halpert

Uncovering Food Insecurity Among College Students, a Tricky Population

It's a cold December day in Ypsilanti, Michigan. Soft snowflakes fall quietly from the sky marking the end of an unseasonably warm fall. On the campus of Eastern Michigan University, students fight their way through the cold, barely glancing up to see if any obstacles block their path. Some of these swift passerby's may be heading to Swoop's, a food pantry located in a nearby university building. Haley Moraniec, a social worker and graduate of Eastern Michigan University, started this on campus food bank back in September of 2015. Inside, shelves are stacked high with canned goods, boxes of cereal and pasta. Three refrigerators containing fresh produce, meat and dairy products line the wall. Red peppers, Greek yogurt, eggs, and even an entire ham are among the selection. All of this is free to students. Moraniec's intention in creating this pantry was to alleviate the burdens students face in terms of food access on her home campus. Considering how diverse Eastern's student population is, Moraniec says that "this is something that our students can greatly benefit from. It's a small part in the fight for food justice."

Efforts like Swoop's are arising in reponse to a growing issue on college campuses: food insecurity, or the lack of access to nutritious food due to financial barriers. The Wisconsin HOPE Lab, an institution dedicated to studying the issues associated with college affordability, recently released a data briefing that detailed their results from a 2015 study. The lab surveyed 1,007 low- and moderate-income students at ten Wisconsin colleges and universities and found that 61 percent were food insecure at some point during the school year. The report also states that 42 percent of respondents said that they cut or skipped meals because they did not have adequate funds. Thirty percent stated that they were hungry but could not afford to eat because they lacked the financial means.

What is even more striking is that according to Sonal Chauhan, Associate Director of Membership and Outreach at the College and University Food Bank Alliance (CUFBA), "the typical food insecure student is working part-time, receives financial aid, and is reaching out for assistance from aid programs – and is still struggling to get by." Without the proper resources on college campuses, students stretch what money they have to cover the costs of their education, living expenses and food. She says, "Studies, including our own recent report, show that a significant percentage of college clients choose between educational expenses, like tuition, textbooks, and rent, versus food."

The choice between allocating funds to food or to educational resources places an unnecessary burden onto students. "It's hard to concentrate in class or focus on your studies when you're hungry or worrying about where your next meal will come from," says Chauhan. In extreme cases, food insecurity can force students to take time off from school or discontinue their education entirely.

Anthony Hernandez, a graduate student working in the Wisconsin HOPE Lab, reinforced Chauhan's statement about the hardships food insecure students suffer. He put it simply: student success is negatively impacted when they don't have their basic needs met. Yet, those who are susceptible to food insecurity are not just students receiving financial aid. "There are other important factors to consider, like students who have medical care costs and may not be covered by insurance in areas where they attend school," says Hernandez. Also, with tuition rising faster than inflation, even financially secure students may be at risk.

The United States Department of Agriculture (USDA) releases an annual report on food insecurity at the national level. Their 2015 findings report that 12.7 percent of American households are food insecure. Yet, according to Alisha Coleman-Jensen, a sociologist at the Economic Research Service of the USDA, nationally representative statistics about college food insecurity are very difficult to capture. As students are often considered part of their parent's households they are viewed as one unit, even if their food situation may vary greatly from when they are at home to when they are at school. "It's difficult to derive a statistic for college students and say it is representative for all students," says Coleman-Jensen, "especially when the age and demographic makeup vary a lot between commuter schools and universities with a more on-campus population."

Smaller scale studies of food insecurity can also prove difficult for researchers. Elena Huisman, a graduate of the University of Michigan with a Masters Degree in Environmental Policy, Planning and Environmental Justice, surveyed 300 plus students at 29 universities in 2014 and found that 24 percent of them were food insecure. This is significantly lower than other studies, but Huisman says that her results may have been skewed because distribution may not have been representative of the entire campus. Huisman also recognizes how unique college populations are in terms of their living situations. From freshmen living in dorms, to seniors living off campus, Huisman says "there are so many different situations found in the college atmosphere that makes determining food access very difficult." Even with lower results, her recommendations still call for action from universities to erase the stigma associated with food insecurity and streamline existing initiatives alleviating student hardships.

Selection of dry goods at Swoop's Food Pantry

As an example of one of these initiatives, Swoop's Food Pantry has been highly successful in the past year, experiencing over a thousand visits composed of almost 500 unique individuals. According to Moraniec, the pantry has received praise for their food assistance efforts as well as becoming a centralized resource for those experiencing other issues like housing instability or domestic violence. The dialogue it has created is very important for campus, says Moraniec. Especially when, she says, "people always ask, well if you can afford college tuition why can't you afford food?" The reality is that many students can't afford food, and they are required to take out loans to pay for their degree. Swoop's and other food pantries across the country are challenging the conventional food system, while giving students more choice and stability.

Winning Essays
Granader Prize for Excellence in Upper-Level Writing (social sciences)

Would You Know It If You Saw It?: Gender Differences in College Students' Ability to Identify Sexual Assault

Meredith Fox

From Sociology 310
Nominated by Kimberly Hess

This essay tackles a complicated and incredibly important topic, campus sexual assault, from a unique and innovative angle. In order to answer her research question regarding whether or not college students are able to identify cases of sexual assault, Meredith undertook an ambitious research project that included both an analysis of legal documents and a survey of UM students. After extensive legal research, she created several scenarios that have been legally defined as sexual assault in the state of Michigan. She then used a survey to measure students' responses to these scenarios and determine if those responses were consistent with the law. Her research was thoroughly conducted, and her methods section in this essay illustrates the care and thought that she put into each step of the research process. In her results section, Meredith presents compelling evidence and clearly organizes her analysis to support her argument that women can more consistently and confidently identify cases of sexual assault than men. She gives evidence from the responses to each scenario that both adds to this overall argument and introduces nuance at the same time. As such, this essay is exceptional in its thorough analysis and clear presentation of a complex research topic and project.

Kimberly Hess

Would You Know It If You Saw It?:
Gender Differences in College Students' Ability to Identify Sexual Assault

Introduction:

Many social scientists have studied the prevalence of sexual assaults on college campuses, exploring what makes college campuses an environment that fosters sexual assault at higher rates than other settings. It has been hard to obtain a good measure on the number of incidences of sexual assault, because the stigma associated with sexual assault and university cover-ups make it a very underreported crime.[1] "The Campus Sexual Assault Study" conducted by the U.S. Department of Justice in 2007 estimated that 1 in 5 women has been sexually assaulted during her time in college.[2] Knowing this, the University of Michigan, in 2015, conducted its own study titled "Campus Climate Survey on Sexual Misconduct", which found that 22.5 percent of undergraduate females and 6.8 percent of males reported experiencing nonconsensual sexual acts.[3] In 2015, the same year as the University of Michigan study, the Association of American Universities conducted its own "Campus Climate Survey on Sexual Assault and Sexual Misconduct", which collected data from students at 27 colleges across the nation. That study similarly found that 23.1 percent of female undergraduate students surveyed indicated that they had experienced sexual assault.[4] These results should be very alarming: students, parents, professors, administrators, and staff at colleges across the nation should be concerned about what it is about the college environment or college-aged people that leads to such high rates of sexual assault. Equally alarming is the fact that despite these numbers, it is a rare occurrence to see a college student prosecuted, let alone convicted, of sexual assault.

---

1 Yung, Corey Rayburn, Concealing campus sexual assault: An empirical examination. Psychology, Public Policy, and Law, Vol 21(1), Feb 2015, 1-9. http://dx.doi.org/10.1037/law0000037

2 Krebs, C.P., Lindquist, C.H., Warner, T.D., Fisher, B.S., & Martin, S.L., The Campus Sexual Assault (CSA) Study. Washington, DC: National Institute of Justice, U.S. Department of Justice. (2007).

3 Results of 2015 University of Michigan Campus Climate Survey On Sexual Misconduct (2015)

4 AAU Campus Climate Survey on Sexual Assault and Sexual Misconduct (2015)

One major limitation of the previously-conducted studies is the potential for inconsistent understandings between the respondents and those conducting the research. Of terms used in the survey questions, such as "consent", "sexual assault"," sexual misconduct", and "taking advantage of". For example, a student could respond that he or she has never had a non-consensual sexual encounter, and then answer survey questions about his or her experiences that would indicate that he or she, in fact, had been engaged in a sexual encounter without giving consent. That student would be counted in the data as having been sexually assaulted, even though he or she did not believe that they were. Virtually no sociological research has been done to better understand how college students define sexual assault and what they believe constitutes an instance of sexual assault. It is particularly interesting to note that while sexual assault appears to be prevalent on college campuses, very few students believe that sexual assault (or misconduct) is a big problem on their campuses or that they are likely to experience it themselves.[5] This suggests there may be some disconnect between what students believe constitutes sexual assault and what is legally considered to be a punishable crime under rape, criminal sexual conduct, sexual misconduct, or sexual assault statutes.[6]

In this study, I explored what University of Michigan students consider to be sexual assault in comparison to what the laws in the State of Michigan consider to be sexual assault. Ultimately, I was able to conclude that, in large part, what University of Michigan students consider to be sexual assault often differs considerably from what can be prosecuted as sexual assault under Michigan law, with the most significant disparity being drawn along gender lines. In this paper, I will argue that gender has the largest impact on whether a student's belief that something is sexual assault is consistent with the law, and, in particular, that females are more likely to identify legally prosecutable criminal sexual acts as sexual assault.

---

5 Id.

6 Different states refer to sexual assault differently, generally calling it rape, criminal sexual conduct, sexual misconduct, or sexual assault.

Method:

The first variable I attempted to study was University of Michigan students' beliefs on what constitutes sexual assault. This was conceptualized by more than just the respondents' definitions of sexual assault. Rather, their beliefs were categorized based on what types of illegal criminal sexual conduct students labeled as sexual assault. The primary method used to measure this variable was survey questions that provided students with six scenarios depicting the following six instances of sexual assault: 1). statutory rape; 2) physically helpless due to alcohol; 3) he said/she said involving alcohol with no physical evidence/injury; 4) he said/she said involving alcohol with substantial physical evidence/injury; 5) male does not consent involving alcohol; and 6) relationship rape. Respondents were asked to identify how likely it was that a sexual assault occurred from the following predetermined choices: definitely, it's likely, it's unlikely, definitely not, and not sure. From how they identified the likeliness that a sexual assault occurred, I could infer what different groups of students generally consider to be sexual assault, and how confident they are in that identification. Additionally, respondents who indicated a sexual assault had definitely occurred were asked how serious of a crime they think it was and what the punishment for the offender should be. For how serious the crime was, respondents were given the following choices: very serious, somewhat serious, not very serious, and not serious at all. The options for what they believed the punishment should be were prison (more than 365 days); jail (less than 365 days); fines, community service; counseling; and other. This provided information on the students' attitudes on the tiers of severity to be compared to the four degrees of severity of sexual assault under Michigan law.

The survey also asked respondents two open-ended questions: 1) to define sexual assault in their own words; and 2) to list synonyms for sexual assault. It was never implied that students should be answering any questions based on what they believe is legal or illegal, so this question was helpful in further determining how students understand and think about sexual assault. The goal of this survey was not simply to quiz students on their knowledge of the law, but rather to see if students generally hold viewpoints about what a sexual assault is that are similar to what the law regards and prosecutes as sexual assault.

One limitation of the survey is that there is no way to tell whether some students answered that scenarios were not sexual assault, even if they knew the act to be illegal, because of their own personal belief that the described act should not be considered illegal. Self-reported data was essential in gaining insight into students' personal beliefs. Surveys generally have less validity than interviews, which I consciously sacrificed for the benefit of being able to see trends and reach conclusions that could be applied more broadly to college students in general. The survey was not intended to capture why students conceptualize sexual assault the way that they do. It is also unknown whether the respondents had received any prior education on the topic, or what experiences may have influenced their beliefs about what is sexual assault and what is not.

Respondents were also asked to rank the severity of the problem of sexual assault on U of M's campus from the following choices: a very big problem, a big problem, somewhat of a problem, and not a problem at all. Previous studies were limited in that they did not examine why students do not think sexual assault is a major problem on their campuses, even when statistically it is. By asking this question in conjunction with learning whether students are able to identify legally recognized instances of sexual assault, it could be determined whether students who do not think sexual assault is a significant problem do not understand what is legally considered sexual assault.

The second variable, the legal definition of sexual assault in Michigan, was somewhat difficult to conceptualize, because laws are constantly being interpreted by the courts. In order to define and conceptualize Michigan law, many documents were analyzed, including the Michigan Penal Code, and dozens of Michigan Appellate and Supreme Court cases. The Michigan Penal Code, MCL 750.520 (b)–(e), defines four degrees of criminal sexual conduct, which is also referred to as rape, sexual assault, or sexual misconduct. Criminal sexual conduct in the first, second, and third degrees are felonies, whereas criminal sexual conduct in the fourth degree is a misdemeanor. All degrees of criminal sexual conduct are punishable with fines, incarceration, or both. Nearly all laws have been further defined by the courts at some point. It is reasonable to conceptualize the law as the decisions of the highest court to address an issue, because according to the doctrine of *stare decisis*, lower courts (like trial courts) have to follow the interpretations of the law as set forth in the opinions of the higher courts. Among the Michigan higher court cases, six different types of prosecutable sex crimes emerged most often: statutory rape; physically helpless due to alcohol; he said/she said involving alcohol with no physical evidence/injury; he said/she said involving alcohol with substantial physical evidence/injury; male does not consent involving alcohol; and relationship rape.

The six scenarios provided were all based upon the central holdings in reported court decisions falling those six categories. For example, Scenario 1 stated: "Shelly is a 14-year-old female and she purposely misrepresents her age to Eli, an 18-year-old male. She tells him that she is 18 and that she wants to have sex with him. The two do have sex. Shelly's parents find out and say she was sexually assaulted, because she is not old enough to consent. Did Eli sexually assault Shelly?" This fact pattern is intended to line up with the central holding in *People v. Adkins* (2006)[7], in which the Michigan Court of Appeals held that a victim's misrepresentation of age does not free a defendant from criminal responsibility, and as such the defendant's conviction of criminal sexual conduct in the third degree was upheld. It is important to note, however, that although fact patterns similar to those provided in the survey have resulted in criminal convictions upheld by higher courts, the chosen sexual assault scenarios have not universally been considered sexual assault in all cases. On rare occasions, higher courts have overturned precedent and laws do change. Nevertheless, it is still valuable to analyze whether students are able to identify instances of supposed sexual assault based on scenarios for which someone could be held criminally responsible today

7 2006 WL 142120

in the State of Michigan. For the purpose of this study, using the definition of Criminal Sexual Conduct in the Michigan Penal Code and the jurisprudence of Michigan higher courts allowed me to categorize a response as having correctly or incorrectly identified something as sexual assault, with "correct" meaning that the response was in accordance with the law.

The survey consisted of two open-ended questions and thirteen objective questions, with the possibility of an additional twelve questions based on a respondent's chosen answer. The survey was made available to a large, unquantifiable number of University of Michigan students. A Qualtrics online survey link was posted in all four University of Michigan Facebook class pages and sent in the Camp Kesem student organization GroupMe, asking students to take the survey themselves and to also send it to friends. Through this combination of convenience and snowball sampling, 89 people responded to at least one survey question, while 61 students completed the survey in its entirety. For the purposes of this paper, only surveys where all questions were answered were considered in the data. Additionally, only responses from students who identified as male or as female were considered, because this research was intended to explore only the disparity between students with those two gender identifications. For this reason, two additional respondents' survey answers were not considered, bringing the total sample to 59 students.

The resulting sample was ultimately not very representative of the population. Females and Democrats were overrepresented, with 78 percent of the respondents identifying as female and 64 percent identifying as Democrats. The distribution among graduation years was nearly even, with 22 percent of the respondents from the class of 2017, 20 percent from the class of 2018, 32 percent from the class of 2019, and 25 percent from the class of 2020. The underrepresentation of males and non-response bias may have some impact on the generalizability, but not the reliability, of the results. Each participant was asked the same questions, and there were very few outliers from the general trends. The lack of response from males makes it more difficult to generalize a trend as to the male student population as a whole. The non-response bias may also have some implications, because, perhaps, people who care more about sexual assault were more likely to respond to a survey on sexual assault. These people would likely be more educated on the topic as compared to the general population.

Table 1. Sample Demographics

#	Answer	%	Count	#	Answer	%	Count	#	Answer	%	Count
1	2017	22.03%	13	1	Republican	15.25%	9	2	Female	77.97%	46
2	2018	20.34%	12	2	Democrat	64.41%	38	1	Male	22.03%	13
3	2019	32.20%	19	3	Independent	20.34%	12		Total	100%	59
4	2020	25.42%	15		Total	100%	59				
	Total	100%	59								

The Qualtrics online survey program did not collect names or any other identifying information to ensure complete confidentiality. Additionally, all respondents had to click that they agreed to participate voluntarily in this study. The participant pool was selected based on whose responses would be necessary to answer the research question. Due to participant anonymity and the sampling method, it cannot be determined whether any non-University of Michigan undergraduates chose to take the survey, even though it requested that only those students complete the survey. In addition, the topic of sexual assault can be sensitive, especially for those who have experienced it. To minimize emotional risk, participants were not asked about any of their personal experiences with sexual assault and all respondents were informed of the confidentiality agreement. Therefore, there would be little reason for someone to answer the questions less than honestly.

Results:

University of Michigan students generally have extreme difficulty in confidently and consistently identifying instances of sexual assault, especially in instances where the male perpetrator denies guilt, the female victim was drinking, or there seems to be a lack of criminal intent on part of a male perpetrator.

However, in all cases, females' identifications are far more in line with the law than males. When given a scenario that mirrors what the Michigan higher courts and Michigan Penal Code have and would consider sexual assault or enough evidence to convict of sexual assault, on average females are 1.4 times more likely to say a sexual assault definitely or likely occurred. Per Michigan law, the key element of every degree of sexual assault is lack of consent.[8] When asked to define sexual assault, 52 percent of females mentioned in their definition that someone did not "consent" or "agree", compared to the 38 percent of males who used those words. The aforementioned data suggests that females better understand sexual assault, and because of this, are better at accurately identifying which scenarios depict sexual assault. This, then, translates into females being more aware of the sexual assault that occurs around them, which is consistent with the fact that 89 percent of female respondents believe sexual assault is a very big or big problem on the University of Michigan's campus, compared to the 46 percent of male respondents who indicated sexual assault is very big or big problem on the University of Michigan's campus.

Finally, in the few instances where students, predominantly female, responded that a sexual assault definitely occurred, they overwhelmingly find the crime to be at least somewhat serious and believe that the punishment should be incarceration. On average, 80 percent of students who indicated that an assault definitely occurred considered the offense to be very serious or somewhat serious, and 81 percent believed the punishment should be either jail or prison. This demonstrates that for the minority of students who have a good understanding as to what constitutes sexual assault, it is a very serious offense. All four degrees of criminal sexual conduct in Michigan are considered to be serious crimes, punishable by significant jail or prison time, so it makes sense that the students who recognize instances of sexual assault find it to be quite serious, because this group is well-educated on the topic of sexual assault. These statistics are limited because since very few males indicated that a sexual assault definitely occurred in

---

8 The Michigan Penal Code Act 328 of 1931 Chapter LXXVI

most scenarios, they were not prompted to answer if they thought it was a serious offense and what the punishment should be.

<u>The Case of Statutory Rape</u>

The weakest identification of an occurrence of sexual assault occurred when students were presented with an underage victim who pretended to be older than she was. In the State of Michigan, "[a] person is guilty of criminal sexual conduct in the third degree if the person engages in sexual penetration with another person and if any of the following circumstances exist: (a) That other person is at least 13 years of age and under 16 years of age...."[9] This is commonly known as statutory rape. In *People v. Adkins* (2006)[10], the Court of Appeals clarified that a victim's misrepresentation of age does not free a defendant of criminal responsibility. The scenario clearly presented that the male was 18 years old and the female was 14 years old, so with confidence, this can be legally considered to be sexual assault.

Figure 1: Identification of Statutory Rape Along Gender Lines

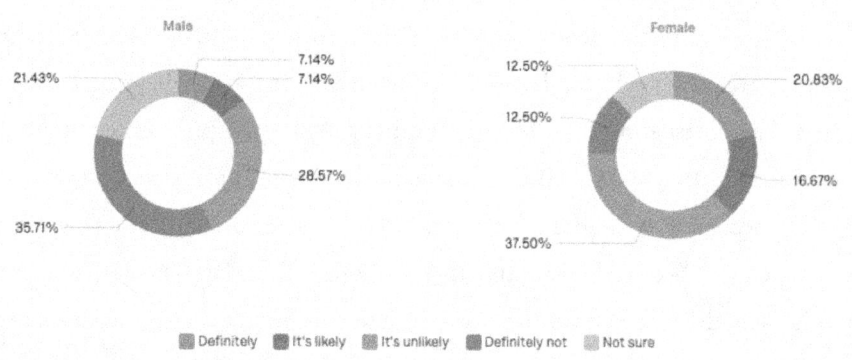

When presented with a very clear-cut scenario of statutory rape, only 7 percent of males believed sexual assault definitely happened, as opposed to the 36 percent of males who said a sexual assault definitely did not occur. Female students did not do much better, with only 21 percent indicating a sexual assault definitely took place. However, only 13 percent of females answered that a sexual

9 MCL 750.520d

10 2006 WL 142120

assault definitely did not occur. The identification was weak in both genders, but males were more confident in saying that an assault definitely did not occur, while females were more likely to say that it was unlikely that an assault occurred. This is demonstrated by the fact that the most common answer for males was definitely not (36 percent), while the most common answer for females was unlikely (38 percent). It is possible that many students knew this act is illegal, but felt it should not be, and so they did not identify it as a sexual assault. However, it is more likely that students are unaware that a sexual assault can occur when the sexual contact is not unwanted and agreed upon by both parties. In their open-ended responses 58 percent of all respondents (54 percent of males and 59 percent of females) indicated that sexual assault is when contact is "unwanted", "against wishes", or "undesired." This suggests that many students, particularly those who are male, believe that a sexual assault occurs only if someone does not want or wish for the sexual contact, even though the statutory rape law does not require contact to be undesired. It would be interesting for further research to examine at what age of a victim respondents draw the line. The age of consent in Michigan is sixteen years of age, and the respondents were presented with a female 2 years under the age of consent. Further research could explore whether respondents still do not believe it is sexual assault when a willing victim is thirteen, twelve, or eleven years old.

Alcohol Related Sexual Assault:

Factoring alcohol into sexual assault scenarios continues to divide respondents along gender lines. Students are most likely to consider an incident sexual assault when alcohol renders the victim too physically helpless to consent. Yet, even in such a scenario, the level of identification is still not that high. When presented with a scenario in which a victim reports having no memory whatsoever and the perpetrator admits the two had sex, the number of students able to identify an assault has occurred is noticeably low. According to the Michigan Penal Code, a criminal sexual act has occurred if the victim is "physically helpless", which is further defined as "a person is unconscious, asleep, or for any other reason is physically unable to communicate unwillingness to an act."[11] The Michigan

11 MCL 750.520a(m)

Court of Appeals, in *People v. Davis* (2014)[12], affirmed that severe intoxication is a form of physical helplessness. However, only 41 percent of all respondents indicated that a sexual assault definitely occurred when presented with a victim too incapacitated by alcohol to have any memory of having had sex at all. Female students were a little more confident in classifying this as sexual assault, as 47 percent of them said it was definitely sexual assault, compared to the 21 percent of male students who responded that it was definitely sexual assault. Incidentally, the same percentage of males (21 percent) indicated that it was unlikely that a sexual assault occurred. With a survey, we are limited in knowing if the respondents did not believe that the female had no memory, if they do not think drinking to the point of not having any memory makes it so that a person is not legally able to consent, or even if they felt that by drinking to the point of having no memory, the female student bore responsibility for the consequences. In any event, less than half of all students and less than a quarter of male students were able to say that an assault definitely occurred.

The sharpest gender division in alcohol-related sexual assault comes with the he said/she said scenario, especially with a lack of physical evidence to suggest force or coercion. When a female was drunk and states that she has memory of not consenting to sex, and there is no physical evidence, most male survey respondents did not believe a sexual assault had occurred. In fact, 21 percent of male respondents said an assault definitely did not occur, compared to 0 percent of females who answered definitely not. It is understandable that far fewer respondents (only 2 percent) answered this scenario with "definitely", because the only physical evidence was that the female's Blood Alcohol Concentration (BAC) of 0.15-- above the 0.08 legal threshold of intoxication in Michigan.[13] It should be noted that the survey did not explain the meaning of Blood Alcohol Concentration, as it was assumed that U of M students would know what this means, although it cannot be ruled out entirely at that some respondents had trouble with this scenario based on a lack of understanding of BAC. Other than

12 2014 Mich. App. LEXIS 1275
13 Michigan Vehicle Code Act 300 of 1949 Section 257.625

the BAC, the only evidence at all was the female accuser's word. The Michigan Penal Code provides, however that "[the testimony of a victim need not be corroborated in prosecutions"[14] in criminal sexual conduct cases, meaning the victim's word alone is enough to convict. This standard was upheld and clarified in *People v. Armijo* (2009)[15], where the Court of Appeals held under that the criminal sexual conduct statute "there is no requirement that physical evidence or eyewitnesses corroborate the victim's testimony. Rather, a victim's uncorroborated testimony is sufficient to convict a defendant…" Obviously, it is reasonable to say the scenario provided in this survey will not be classified as criminal sexual conduct 100 percent of the time, because the jury decides if the witness seems credible on the stand. However, an interesting conclusion that can be drawn from the responses to this scenario is that rather than select the provided option of unsure, because respondents did not get to assess in person the credibility of the witness, a majority of male respondents (57 percent) indicated it was unlikely an assault took place or that an assault definitely did not take place, even though in the scenario the female victim went to a hospital and told the doctors that she did not consent to having sex. More than half of male respondents were unwilling to take her at her word. On the other hand, a majority of female respondents believed the victim, or marked unsure. The subsequent scenarios provided further data affirming that males are not likely to believe a female accuser, especially when alcohol is involved.

Even in the face of substantial physical evidence of injury, respondents, particularly males, had a very difficult time characterizing an incident as sexual assault when alcohol was involved and the male says he did not do it. Only 6 percent of all respondents said that a sexual assault definitely occurred, even when told that the victim remembers saying no, went to a hospital, had a positive rape kit, and had "severe bleeding and bruising." A majority of female respondents indicated that it was likely a sexual assault occurred, whereas male respondents were pretty split without a majority selecting any single answer choice. This

---

14 Michigan Penal Code 750.520h

15 2009 WL 2974759

scenario is very similar to the one in the previous paragraph, except this scenario provided evidence of physical injuries ("severe bruising and bleeding"), yet respondents were not more likely to confidently label this as sexual assault. In fact, they seemed even more unsure when the physical injuries were added, with 36 percent of all respondents answering unsure, compared to the previous scenario without physical injury where only 25 percent were unsure. It is worth noting that far more males were unsure in this instance (31 percent), as compared to how many were unsure in the scenario with no physical evidence of injury (7 percent). The only difference in these scenarios that could possibly account for the increase in male uncertainty is that in the scenario with physical evidence, the male defendant much more firmly asserted that he did not rape the female, whereas in the previous scenario of no physical injury, the male denied that accusation, but not as vehemently. There should be no reason to be more unsure when more evidence against the perpetrator is added, so the only explanation is that males are more inclined to believe other males over females. When presented with the medical evidence in conjunction with information that the male adamantly denies guilt, males still cannot side with the female, but they feel conflicted when presented with significant physical evidence. They thus mark unsure, solidifying their unwillingness to believe a female victim.

Male Victim:

The type of criminal sexual conduct that students were most able to identify as sexual assault was a woman sexually assaulting a man. 100 percent of respondents said that the male was definitely or likely sexually assaulted, with most responding with definitely. The scenario indicates that the male neither clearly consented, nor clearly said no. It also reports that he was drunk and aroused. Yet, more than any of the scenarios involving women being assaulted, respondents were overwhelmingly more accurate in characterizing this as sexual assault. This shows a sharp contrast between drunk female and male accusers, because males are far more likely to believe a drunk male who says he was raped. It seems both genders are acutely aware that a male can be a victim and a female a perpetrator of sexual assault. When asked "Do you believe that if a male and female are both severely intoxicated and have sex that it is ever possible that one sexually assaulted the other?" 100 percent of males and 98 percent of females indicated that it is both possible for the male to sexually assault the female and for the female to sexually assault the male. Even though sexual assault of females is far more prevalent, people are still better at identifying instances where a male is sexually assaulted. It seems that males are considered more believable than females by students at large, but especially by other males.

Relationship Rape:

Exactly half of all survey respondents were able to classify relationship rape as sexual assault. Relationship rape was defined in this instance as two people who live together and are in a relationship that has been of a sexual nature, but nevertheless one night the female does not wish to have sex and repeatedly tells her male partner no while pushing him away. He overcomes her and has sex with her. The definition of criminal sexual conduct in the third degree in the Michigan Penal Code provides that an assault has occurred if "force or coercion is used to accomplish the sexual penetration."[16] A separate section specifically clarifies that even when two people are married, one can still be found guilty of raping the other.[17]

Figure 2: Relationship Rape Along Gender Lines

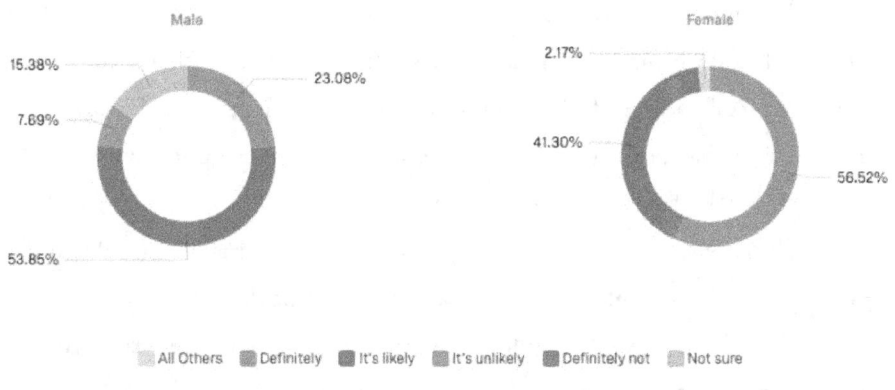

---

16 MCL 520d(1)(b)
17 MCL 720.5201

This scenario, however, highlighted a clear disconnect, because even when the legal standard for this type of rape is very clear and so is the scenario, students are less than confident in labeling it as an occurrence of sexual assault, with 44 percent answering likely instead of definitely. Even more surprising, 8 percent of males (compared to 2 percent of females) indicated that it is unlikely that a sexual assault took place, while 15 percent of males (and 0 percent of females) said they were unsure whether a sexual assault took place. This survey is limited in the sense that I cannot conclude whether this discrepancy is due to ignorance of or disagreement with the law. In any event, for one reason or the other, many students do not identify relationship rape as definitely sexual assault, even when force and coercion is present. This trend is consistent among many scenarios, which are clearly sexual assault under the law.

Conclusion:

Overall, University of Michigan students' beliefs about what constitutes sexual assault are drastically different from what the law in the State of Michigan considers to be sexual assault. The biggest discrepancies in ability to identify legally recognizable sexual assault are drawn along gender lines, where being male has a strong negative correlation. When presented with six common types of sexual assault (statutory rape, physically helpless due to alcohol, he said/she said involving alcohol with no physical evidence/injury, he said/she said involving alcohol with substantial physical evidence/injury, male does not consent involving alcohol, and relationship rape), males are less likely to conclude that sexual assault definitely or likely occurred. Difficulties in identification arise particularly when a female victim has been drinking, a male assailant denies guilt, or when there seems to be a lack of criminal intent.

Ultimately, students, especially those who are male, considered few legally prosecutable acts of criminal sexual conduct to be definitely, or even likely, sexual assault. With sexual assault so prevalent and grossly underreported on college campuses, it is important for us to recognize that students do not really understand what constitutes sexual assault. College-aged females are particularly vulnerable to being sexually assaulted by college-aged males. For this reason, it is very relevant to that female students might not know to report something that happened to them, because they do not understand it is an assault. Perhaps even more problematic, male students may commit acts of sexual assault, because they do not know what they are doing is illegal. Many male respondents were unable to identify even the clearest illustrations of sexual assault and, correspondingly, were far more likely to think that sexual assault is not really a problem on this campus.

The University of Michigan is certainly not the only college with both sexual assault and underreporting problems. The Association of American Universities survey conducted at 27 colleges across the nation found that 23.1 percent of female undergraduates experience sexual assault, and of those, only 5-28 percent are reported.[18] Due to the fact that the results of the University of Michigan's own sexual assault and reporting rates were remarkably similar to the AAU's 2007 study, the results of this research are likely generalizable to many other similar universities. There could be other factors, such as the presence or lack of alcohol on campus, Greek life, and access to bars, that could impact whether these results are applicable to all colleges, but they are likely relevant to similar institutions. This study contributes to the understanding of why sexual assault is so prevalent on college campuses by suggesting that it can be attributed at least in part to a serious lack of understanding on the part of students as to what constitutes sexual assault. It is particularly concerning that male students identify instances of sexual assault at alarmingly low rates, because this suggests that many males who commit sexual assault might honestly believe that they are not committing a crime.

Further research should explore qualitatively why many respondents did not find many instances of criminal sexual conduct to be likely or definitely sexual assault. This study was not able to identify why there was the gender discrepancy in identification of sexual assault, or what led to the overall mismatch between the law and students' perceptions of the law. It would also be beneficial to look

---

18 AAU Campus Climate Survey on Sexual Assault and Sexual Misconduct (2015)

into discrepancies between male and female education on sexual assault to explore its potential impact on the gender discrepancy in classifying sexual assault. In addition, exploring more generally what type of education students have received on sexual assault might help explain why they hold varying beliefs about what constitutes sexual assault in comparison to the legal standards. This research would allow educators to create and implement more effective sexual assault education programming for students. It is imperative that college administrators make sexual assault education a priority to address the clear differences in what can and will be legally prosecuted as sexual assault versus what students consider to be sexual assault.

Chapter 1: The Characters

Michael Gawlik

From History 499

Nominated by John Carson

Michael Gawlik's "The Characters" is a smart and engaging analysis of three genres of writing about prostitution in 19th-century America. In this chapter Michael identifies the central character "roles" that he found in his examination of various genres of writing about prostitution. The roles include the "rural girl," "wealthy boy," "mother," "madam," and "the public." Michael engagingly describes what each of these roles entailed as they were used in various forms of middle-class writing (anti-prostitution literature, sensationalist magazines, and novels) typically to construct a story about a girl's fall into prostitution and who should be blamed for this event. More than just describe these roles, however, Michael also explores how 19th-century audiences would have responded to them, pointing out shrewdly places where traditional moral sensibilities and the ambiguities of the narratives would have come into tension. Throughout one sees demonstrated Michael's deft ability to put together material from a wide range of sources to construct a convincing and compelling argument.

John Carson

The Brothel on the Page:

Print, Prostitution, and Blame in Antebellum America

CHAPTER ONE: The Characters

"Another Ellen Jewett Affair" had transpired in Boston, declared a *National Police Gazette* headline in November 1845. Evoking memories of the infamous New York City brothel murder that created shockwaves throughout the country almost a decade prior, the *Gazette* narrated to its audience of 15,000 readers a case from Massachusetts that bore eerie parallels to its predecessor. As in the Jewett case, the so-called "Boston Murder" saw a prostitute, Maria A. Bickford, slain by the hand of her lover, one Albert J. Tirrell.[1]

As it did in any number of stories about prostitutes whose lives were destroyed by their paramours, the *Gazette* spoke with apparent outrage on behalf of the fallen woman. Advertising a $3,000 reward for the capture of Tirrell, the paper demanded that such a man, whose "character is entirely without relief, his case entirely undeserving of sympathy," be brought to justice so he could never again contribute to the antebellum city's growing "dark catalogue of homicides." In coverage of the ensuing 1846 trial for murder, the *Gazette* continued its campaign against Tirrell, decrying his artifice as being the cause of Maria Bickford's ruin. Not only had the man lured Bickford away from her husband and into a life of prostitution, but he also brought about her brutal end by taking a razor to her throat. Anything less than a guilty verdict was unacceptable to the *Gazette;* Tirrell was, in the newspaper's conception, nothing less than a heinous villain.[2]

Though spectacular and provocative, Maria Bickford's story was far from singular in antebellum print culture. Seemingly everyone in the antebellum world, from newspapermen looking to profit from their enterprises, to moral reformers seeking to return God to the center of urban life, to sensationalist novelists aiming to arouse and titillate their readers, had something to write about prostitution.

---

1 The National Police Gazette covers Bickford's murder extensively from late 1845 to 1846, providing reports of the crime, information about the backgrounds of its victim and perpetrator, details of court proceedings, and opinions regarding the case. "Another Ellen Jewett Affair," National Police Gazette, November 1, 1845.

2 "The Boston Murder," National Police Gazette, November 15, 1845; "The Boston Tragedy," National Police Gazette, April 4, 1846.

Though reasons for writing about commercial sex were diverse, prostitution narratives of the period, which tended to blend fact and fiction under a façade of authenticity, shared a remarkably consistent trajectory: a girl from the countryside meets a young man of means; he takes her virginity, then abandons her to a brothel in the city; after living a life of degradation for some time, the girl dies alone.[3] These stories were not, however, mere duplicates of one another. While the plot of prostitution narratives is constant and the cast of characters recurring—in addition to the seduced and the seducer, stories almost always feature oblivious families that lurk on the periphery, hawkeyed brothel madams that aim to profit from young girls' ruin, and a society composed of people complicit in, unknowing of, or actively fighting against commercial sex—significant differences exist in the ways that narratives assign blame for prostitution.

Historian Andie Tucher has argued that two distinct narrative patterns exist in antebellum era prostitution stories. The first, known as the Poor Unfortunate narrative, regards seduced girls as victims of deceit and trickery, while the second, the Siren narrative, consider girls to be prostitutes by choice, who purposely disregard values of virtue and restraint in pursuit of sin.[4] Both narratives assign blame to a single actor; in Poor Unfortunate stories, at fault are the wealthy young men who lure naïve girls into prostitution, while in Siren stories, prostitutes themselves are to blame for their own wretched behavior.

While Tucher provides a worthwhile framework for considering the ways in which blame could be assigned to different characters in similar stories, most prostitution narratives escape the dualism of her paradigm. Few cases assign blame neatly to either the seducer or the seduced; even Maria Bickford's case, as will be discussed, had a more complicated pattern of blaming than is apparent on the story's surface. Most often, narratives diffuse blame for prostitution among multiple characters, often by using subtext to overtly blame one party for a girl's decline to prostitution while covertly faulting another. Moreover, it is not only

---

3 Timothy J. Gilfoyle, City of Eros: New York City, Prostitution, and the Commercialization of Sex, 1790-1920 (New York: Norton, 1992), 146-148.

4 Andie Tucher, Froth & Scum: Truth, Beauty, Goodness, and the Ax Murder in America's First Mass Medium (Chapel Hill: University of North Carolina Press, 1994), 63.

the seduced girls and seducer boys of prostitution narratives who are placed at fault; a host of other characters can be blamed as well. By exploiting assumptions about propriety and respectability common among middling classes during the antebellum era, narratives inspired fear about culpability for prostitution in all segments of society.

Understanding the images authors created to provoke public interest in and fear about prostitution allows for a more complete understanding of what values Americans felt were threatened by commercial sex's existence. Blame, in particular, is useful for understanding the ways in which these values varied for different segments of society, as it was a designation determined arbitrarily and in accordance with an author and reader's perspective.

This essay provides an overview of the roles that each character played in antebellum narratives, with particular attention paid to how these depictions tapped into popular ideologies and anxieties in order to allocate blame. In describing the role that various characters were shown in perpetuating prostitution, the shifting nature of blame becomes apparent. After expanding on existing scholarly analyses of seduced girls and seducer boys, the essay will explore the little discussed roles that family, brothel madams, and the public each played in popular representations of prostitution.

Rural Girls

"Lured from home, kept for a time, and turned to perish in a brothel," seduced girls are central to stories about prostitution.[5] Without these so-called "fallen women," a story would have no vehicle for explaining how prostitutes came to their unfortunate end, or for exploring who could be put at fault for their condition.

Despite her title, the archetypal "fallen woman" of antebellum narratives begins her descent into prostitution while still a girl. In these stories, victims of seduction are seldom older than eighteen, and could be as young as nine at the

---

5 "The Anniversary of the Female Moral Reform Society,--Sad Condition of the 8th Ward," The New York Herald, May 12, 1842, from Chronicling America: Historic American Newspapers digital database, through the Library of Congress (accessed May 17, 2016).

time of their fall.[6] A girl's youth does not, however, make her sexual impropriety inconsequential. In fact, immediately after being convinced, tricked, or otherwise seduced into having sex, the direction of a girl's life is entirely altered. Her development into a respectable woman truncates. No longer can she hope to live virtuously, or even normally; no longer can she freely associate with her family, or return to the community from which she came. Though she might "recall to mind her heart-broken mother—her brothers and sisters—and weep," the path of depravity that a prostitute has set herself upon is inescapable.[7] Tears and regret cannot regain family or a life of virtue, so a girl must resign herself to living out the remainder of her life in vice.

That prostitution narratives portray the victims of seduction as girls on the precipice of adulthood, whose indiscretion affects the remainder of their lives, is significant. In effect, this representation draws reader attention to the crucial juncture that girls faced as they approached adulthood in antebellum America. This was a time of increasing migration within the United States: a decline in available land and opportunity in rural New England compelled many young Americans to leave behind their provincial birthplaces in search of work in one of the country's growing cities.[8] A girl's transition to womanhood, then, often brought about a move away from home. With this move came a degree of autonomy, as, for likely the first time in her life, a girl lived outside of the purview of her parents, and was free to behave as she wished.

To a cautious and concerned antebellum reader, that autonomy—limited though it would be for young, working women—was particularly troublesome. Rural Americans during this period already regarded cities like New York and Boston with mingled fear and distaste, and accounts reporting that girls in the city could neglect going to church and instead attend balls four times a week likely

---

6 An account in the Advocate of Moral Reform reports on a number of girls between the ages of nine and eleven who work in the third tier of urban theaters, one of the most exchange places of commercial sex in the antebellum city. "Juvenile Thieves and Prostitutes," Advocate of Moral Reform, September 15, 1838.

7 George Thompson, The Gay Girls of New-York, Or, Life on Broadway Being a Mirror of the Fashions, Follies and Crimes of a Great City, (New York: 1853), 12.

8 Catherine E. Kelly, In the New England Fashion: Reshaping Women's Lives in the Nineteenth Century (Ithaca, N.Y.: Cornell University Press, 1999), 1-4.

exacerbated their concerns about daughters living away from home.[9] Additionally, not only did girls in the city face these temptations, but they also encountered them at precisely the age that prostitution narratives suggested a girl was most vulnerable to seduction.

Prostitution narratives' depiction of seduced girls, then, tapped into American fears about children leaving home during the antebellum era. In these stories, readers found a frightening image of what could happen to their own daughters that went to the city. How could readers be sure that the virtue instilled in their children at home wouldn't be wiped away by the vice of the city? How could they know that their daughters would not become another of the "young women from the countryside, destitute of home, friends and work," who found herself "compelled to adopt [the] repulsive and abhorrent profession" of prostitution?[10] A girl becoming a prostitute after moving to the city was the manifestation of rural parents' fears for their daughter: outside of their purview, she would fall into vice and sin.

Moreover, by portraying a girl's entire destiny as being dependent upon the decisions she makes at sixteen or seventeen, prostitution narratives made the consequences of a girl's behavior immediately salient to parents. It tasked them with determining potential sources of a girl's decline into prostitution, and removing these influences from her life before she left for the city and did harm to her virtue. In order to do this, readers looked to accounts to determine the decisions and influences that led girls to their falls.

Reading is the cause most commonly cited as leading a girl to a seducer. Inheriting a tradition dating to antiquity, antebellum Americans believed reason and emotion to be cognitive capacities existing on a gendered binary, with men having domain over the former while women dealt in the latter. Because of the two capacities' irreconcilable nature, only one could be engaged at a time; novel reading was an activity that stimulated emotion, rather than reason. Women, then, were the sex more likely to indulge in fiction reading, for it suited the cognitive

9 "Female Labor," National Police Gazette, April 3, 1847.
10 George G. Foster, New York by Gas-Light: With Here and There a Streak of Sunshine (New York: Dewitt & Davenport, 1850),17.

capacity thought to be inherent to them. While in moderation novels could provide a woman an opportunity to practice empathy, excessive consumption of fiction made her self-absorbed and capricious.[11] Romantic fantasies would develop in the heart of a reader, causing her to engage in thoughtless behavior motivated by what she saw in novels rather than what is reasonable in the real world. A novel, then, was capable of leading a girl to danger. As Reverend John Bennett, author of a popular late eighteenth century exposition on female education and intellect, described, novels "inflame [women's] fancy, and effectively pave the way for their seduction."[12]

In a world that Americans believed was filled with prostitution, then, having a voracious reader for a daughter would be frightening. What would stop a girl from fantasizing that she might have a life like the ones about which she reads in books? What would stop her from attempting to make her fantasized life a reality? Romance, in particular, was a genre feared for encouraging the desires that would lead a girl directly into the arms of a seducer. "The libertine and the writer of romance are near akin," suggested an article in the *Advocate of Moral Reform* that described how books cause girls to lose interest in the sober pursuits of daily life and instead dream of romance.[13] Bored by their condition and given a peek into a life infinitely more alluring than their own, romance novels could persuade girls to abandon a life of virtue and domesticity for the promise of love that a seducer offers.

Should a girl find herself in the company of a seducer, her chance of escaping his grasp before he initiated her sexual ruin is doubtful. Antebellum print sources continually insist on a girl's inability to effectively judge good character in men, and advice abounds of the types of men she should avoid. "Ride, walk, sit, associate with no men, whose conduct has been such, as in a female, would cause

---

11 Mary Kelley, "Genres of Print: Introduction," in An Extensive Republic: Print, Culture, and Society in the New Nation, 1790-1840, ed. Robert A. Grossman and Mary Kelley (Chapel Hill: Published in association with the American Antiquarian Society by the University of North Carolina Press, 2010), 386; Helen Lefkowitz Horowitz, Rereading Sex: Battles over Sexual Knowledge and Suppression in Nineteenth-Century America (New York: Alfred A. Knopf : Distributed by Random House, 2002), 43-44.

12 John Bennett, Strictures on Female Education, Chiefly as It Relates to the Culture of the Heart, in Four Essays (Philadelphia, 1793), 77, via Kelley, "Genres of Print: Introduction," 386.

13 "To Novel Readers," The Advocate of Moral Reform, July 1, 1837.

you to avoid her society," warns one account in the *Advocate*.[14] The omnipresence of such advice in print sources (particularly reform periodicals) suggests that girls were seen as unable to discern for themselves whether or not a man was a seducer. Unaware of his duplicitous nature, how could a girl escape his company before succumbing to his advances?

Indeed, many of the girls who appear in prostitution narratives appear to be of good character despite their impending, or already realized, ruin. In George Thompson's *The Gay Girls of New-York*, a sensationalist novel chronicling the happenings of a brothel and its occupants, prostitute Hannah Sherwood is described as possessing "the praiseworthy attributes of generosity and humanity." Hannah helps defend other girls from seduction in hopes that they don't reach the same fate she has, proving herself to be a kind, if sometimes mischievous, fallen woman. Thompson even recognizes that readers might be surprised to find he characterizes a prostitute so positively, but contends, "The loss of virtue in a woman does not necessarily involve the destruction of all the good qualities of her nature."[15]

Accounts such as this make clear, then, that some prostitutes are not merely sirens who intentionally set themselves upon a path of depravity in order to engage in a life of sin. Many are merely women whose naïveté and distance from home caused them to fall for a man's seduction. The *National Police Gazette* typically upheld this characterization of prostitutes, lamenting a girl's fall and expressing regret at her inevitable death in pointedly titled articles such as "Suicide of a Young and Beautiful Girl, Produced by Infamy and Deceit."[16] In these stories, girls do not pursue lives of prostitution, but rather are forced into them by bad men.

Does a girl's lack of desire to become a prostitute, however, absolve her entirely from guilt for her condition? Many accounts suggest it does not. Though

14 "Run, Speak to that young Woman," The Advocate of Moral Reform, February 15, 1837.
15 Thompson, The Gay Girls of New-York, 22.
16 "Suicide of a Young and Beautiful Girl, produced by Deceit and Infamy," National Police Gazette, May 30, 1846.

the *Advocate of Moral Reform* recognizes that girls might have had no intention of becoming prostitutes, it contends that they still carry some of the blame for their seduction. "I firmly believe that in ninety-nine cases out of an hundred," concluded a front-page article of an 1838 issue, "the seduced meets the seducer, if not half-way, yet a considerable distance, in consequence of the previous corruption of her heart." [17] Girls had, after all, been given plenty of warning about the dangers that might put them at risk of seduction. Reading, keeping bad company, and dressing provocatively were all hazardous behaviors in which girls were told not to engage.[18] Furthermore, if seduced girls enjoyed reading so much, how could they have missed the advice against these activities that was so pervasive in print? They did not miss these warnings, the *Advocate* suggested—instead, they engaged in the precise behaviors they were cautioned against out of indulgence and recklessness. Even the *National Police Gazette,* which does not share the *Advocate's* predilection towards scrutinizing a girl's behavior, noted tendencies of improper dress or reading in fallen women.[19]

In the subtext of many prostitution narratives, at least partial blame is placed on girls for their decline. Though accounts are not as harsh on girls as they are on others, they still do not represent these characters as being entirely innocent; a girl's willful disregard for the advice and guidance she is provided "lowers her in [a seducer's] estimation and encourages him to hope that once again he may be successful in his scheme of darkness."[20] In essence, these accounts suggest that a girl leads herself to the brink of seduction, where the task of her ruin then falls to the seducer.

But readers were unlikely to wait with baited breath to learn whether or not a man was "successful in his scheme of darkness." After all, a prostitution narrative couldn't go on without a man to carry on a girl's fall.

---

17 "Connection Between the Vices No. 2," The Advocate of Moral Reform, December 15, 1838.
18 "Connection Between the Vices No. 2," The Advocate of Moral Reform, December 15, 1838.
19 "Interesting Particulars of the Murdered Female in Boston," National Police Gazette (via the Boston Mail), November 8, 1845.
20 "Run, Speak to that young Woman," The Advocate of Moral Reform, February 15, 1837.

Wealthy Boys

Because a young man's sexual advances are presented as being a necessary component of a woman's descent to infamy, it is not surprising that these men are often placed at the center of blame in prostitution stories. More than any other character, young, wealthy men who take on the role of seducer are overtly labeled as being at fault for prostitution. Even accounts from the *Advocate*, which was quite open to blaming girls themselves, placed fault on these men; as the periodical describes, "Painting the character of the seducer in colors too dark....can never be done."[21] This sentiment likely came from the active role that these men took in prostitution narratives; they are the ones who carry out the irreversible step of taking a girl's virginity. Because they play such a crucial role in a girls' downfall, it is almost impossible for authors not to assign fault to these men.

Who are the men that seduce young girls? In most accounts, they are the sons of privilege and respectability. And like the girls they come to seduce, these men are typically from a rural background. In many ways, representations of boys who become seducers tap into the same fears that representations of girls who become prostitutes did: both boys and girls are new arrivals in the city, are living away from parental supervision, and are thus at incredible risk of being drawn into the world of vice and sin. While for girls that risk is of becoming prostitutes themselves, for boys, it is of becoming the men who seduce girls and lead them to prostitution.

A particular fear of parents with boys living in the city came because of the young, male sporting culture developing during the second quarter of the nineteenth century. Unsupervised boardinghouses where fellows of similar age and social standing stayed after moving to the city were the places where this culture developed. In a sense, boardinghouses for young men were the masculine counterparts to brothels for young women—both were represented in print as spaces where people of like morals came together, and accounts often made no distinction between the two.[22] In male boardinghouses, away from the influence

---

21 "Connection Between the Vices No. 2," The Advocate of Moral Reform, December 15, 1838.

22 There were also boardinghouse for women, and stories often fail, perhaps intentionally, to note whether or not these are places of commercial sex. "Grand Larceny," National Police Gazette, January 23, 1847.

of family and home, a culture idealizing bachelorhood and sexual leisure arose. For these sporting men, unrestrained sexuality was an expression of identity, and antebellum courting rituals a threat to their way of life. They frequented dance halls and theaters, both common zones of commercial sex, and were free to do as they pleased in a growing city where consequences for bad behavior were seemingly nonexistent. Having no desire to marry, due both to its increasing cost and because the influence women asserted over the domestic sphere threatened the virility they cultivated around themselves, sporting men turn to brothels. In a prostitute, or a young girl that could be seduced and then tossed aside, these men found an opportunity for sexual gratification that occurred on their own terms, rather than those of their parents or antebellum propriety.[23]

Boys arriving in the city would almost certainly move to one of the boardinghouses where sporting culture was forming. The apprentice system, which had previously allowed transplanted young men to live with their employers in traditional domestic arrangements, largely collapsed in the northeastern United States following the War of 1812, making boardinghouses the primary place for young men to live.[24] Parents, then, might be concerned that their sons would become taken with the licentious lifestyle of their roommates; it was these peers' influence that was believed to draw boys into a life of frequenting brothels. "The young man of twenty to twenty-three of lewd and lecherous habits often becomes the teacher and guide of the soft and unsuspecting lad from fifteen to seventeen," warns an account in the *Advocate*.[25] The story that follows this declaration, which details the son of a respectable clergyman's first foray into a brothel, proved to parents that even boys instilled with the best values could be tempted into sin. These boys would then become the "Foes of Society," as a Boston minister christened men who practiced sexual immorality, who, despite being women's "natural guardians and protectors" destroyed girls in their unquenchable lust.[26]

---

23 Gilfoyle, City of Eros, Chapter 5: Sporting Men; Horowitz, Rereading Sex, 87, 125-128, 139-143; Patricia Cline Cohen, The Murder of Helen Jewett: The Life and Death of a Prostitute in Nineteenth-Century New York (New York: Vintage Books, 1999, 11-12.

24 Gillian Hamilton, "The Decline of Apprenticeship in North America: Evidence from Montreal," The Journal of Economic History 60, no. 3 (2000): 628-629; Cohen, The Murder of Helen Jewett, 11.

25 , "The Rescue of the Innocent from the brink of Ruin," The Advocate of Moral Reform, September 1, 1838.

26 "Strong but Just," National Police Gazette, January 9, 1847.

In the same way that a rake could seduce a girl into prostitution, he could influence a boy to take up a life of sin. Much as girls are doomed to spend the rest of their lives in depravity following seduction, boys "quickly and easily…become ensnared and corrupted" by the world of vice to which their peers introduce them.[27] The consequences of a boy's sexual indiscretion, however, are considerably lower than they are for a girl. Though he might become a "foe of society" and a shame to his family, seducer boys are not predestined to the early and terrible death that seduced girls are—and most often, they are not even held responsible for their behavior.[28]

Though seducers are the party most overtly blamed for prostitution in antebellum narratives, the lack of consequence they face for their sins underscores the subtle ways in which authors often excused their behavior. The most defining feature of this trend is the frequent omission of a seducer's name in accounts. Though scholars have suggested that the authors of some sources, like the *Advocate,* relished the opportunity to publish the names of seducers, in actuality sources very seldom did this, instead referring to these men merely by their first initial or as "villains."[29] Even the *National Police Gazette*, which generally presented itself as sympathetic to the seduced and critical of the seducer, does this regularly; in the piece, "Effects of Seduction," a physician who seduced a twenty-two year old and abandoned her, pregnant, in New York goes unnamed.[30] Meanwhile, the name of the girl, Julia Thompson, is reported in full. Seeing as this story came directly to the *Gazette* from Thompson herself, it seems unlikely that the man's name was omitted because it was unknown—instead, the author hides the name deliberately, shielding the man's identity and reputation while condemning his

---

27 , "The Rescue of the Innocent from the brink of Ruin," The Advocate of Moral Reform, September 1, 1838.

28 In my readings, I have never once come across a story in which a seducer dies an extraordinary or early death. More often, men like Albert Tirrell or Richard Robinson, Helen Jewett's murderer, are shown to escape punishment and return to lives of normalcy.

29 My own findings contradict those of Carroll Smith Rosenberg, as I have read very few accounts that name seducers. More often, it seems that the threat of exposing these men, which is seen in penny press papers of the period as well, is more common than actually doing so. Carroll Smith Rosenberg, "Beauty, the Beast and the Militant Woman: A Case Study in Sex Roles and Social Stress in Jacksonian America," American Quarterly 23, no. 4 (1971): 572-574. For examples of articles that do not name the seducer, see: "Characters in Real Life," The Advocate of Moral Reform, December 15, 1838; "The Rescue of the Innocent from the brink of Ruin," The Advocate of Moral Reform, September 1, 1838.

30 "Effects of Seduction," National Police Gazette, January 9, 1847.

actions. Moreover, the inclusion of Thompson's name forces her into the center of the unsavory story, making only her endure public knowledge of her sexual impropriety.

Even though accounts like this do not outwardly blame women for their fall—men are the visibly condemned party—it still burdens them most with the consequences of sexual sin. The subtext of these pieces is that boys from the countryside who become seducers can continue on with their lives after they have ruined a girl, whose fate, alternatively, is sealed. Death does not hang over a young man's ventures into a brothel as it does for a young woman. Because they face no consequence for their sin, fault leveled against seducers slips away in these accounts. In place of these men, then, authors find new characters to blame for prostitution. In particular, attention shifted onto the ways in which women could lead one another to the brothel, and how mothers could be responsible for a girl's descent into prostitution.

Mothers

Because depictions of the seduced and the seducer in prostitution narratives tapped so deeply into the anxieties that Americans felt about ongoing shifts in migration, family structure, and autonomy during the antebellum period, it would only be natural for parents reading these accounts to wonder what role they themselves might play in a child's ruin. Surely, the families of those girls and boys who went wrong could not have brought them up properly, readers could assure themselves—but just in case, it would not hurt to see what accounts had to say about a family's role in a child's descent.

These readers would certainly not have had to search long to find material that would help them determine their place in a prostitution story. Accounts frequently entertain questions of what might have become of a prostitute if she had been raised differently, forcing readers to consider the ways in which an improper family could be to blame for a prostitute's condition. In particular, the moral character and parenting abilities of mothers was a topic of frequent exploration. "It is hardly too much to say," the *Advocate of Moral Reform* boldly declared in an 1840 article that typified the periodical's emphasis on a mother's duty to her children, "that the mother, under God, holds in her hands the eternal destinies of her child."[31]

This is a constant refrain in the *Advocate*: God has provided mothers with an immense responsibility in caring for their children. The ideology scholars have referred to as Republican Motherhood—the responsibility of mothers to instill morality and good values in their husbands and children in order to uphold societal decency—was deeply at work in the *Advocate's* rhetoric.[32] For instance, the *Advocate* frequently published the constitutions of auxiliaries to the Female Moral Reform Society (the organization that produced the periodical), which consistently included a clause dedicated to describing a mother's obligation to properly instructing her children.[33] Nary a page of the periodical could be read without finding a reference to the responsibilities of Republican Mothers in ensuring the good character of their children.

Both empowering and accusing implications arise out of the *Advocate's* unfaltering support of this ideology. In one sense, this assertion suggested to mothers reading the periodical that they had the privilege and power to affect the moral state of society—after all, "No class in the community exert so powerful an influence in controlling the morals and destinies of the rising generation as mothers." [34] The future was theirs to determine; by teaching morality in the home, a woman ensured her children would enact virtuous living as they made their way into public life. On the other hand, however, Republican Motherhood placed the burden of all societal evils on women. Had these women better instructed their

---

31 "On the Early Religious Education of Children," The Advocate of Moral Reform, February 15, 1840.

32 Richard A. Meckel, "Educating a Ministry of Mothers: Evangelical Maternal Associations, 1815-1860," Journal of the Early Republic 2, no. 4 (1982): 403–404, 422; Linda Kerber, "The Republican Mother: Women and the Enlightenment-An American Perspective," American Quarterly 28, no. 2 (1976): 202–205.

33 The sources provided here is by no means an exhaustive list of all auxiliary constitutions that include clauses about mothers' responsibilities, but are a representative sample. Rachel Robinson, "For the Advocate of Moral Reform: Ferrisburgh Chapter Constitution," The Advocate of Moral Reform, July 1, 1837; J.M. Parker, "For the Advocate of Moral Reform: Chenango Chapter Constitution," The Advocate of Moral Reform, February 1, 1837; "For the Advocate of Moral Reform: Heath Chapter Constitution," The Advocate of Moral Reform, November 15, 1836.

34 Questions for Discussion at Maternal Meetings," The Advocate of Moral Reform, February 15, 1837.

children, vice and sin would not exist to the wide extent in antebellum society that print sources suggested it did.

In this framework, the mother of a prostitute became the target of direct blame for her daughter's condition. By affirming the power of influence a mother had—that "No mother who does her duty in the nursery, and properly manages the young immortals committed to her care, will ever lose the influence which God and nature have given her over the minds and hearts of her children"—the *Advocate* also maintained that children gone wrong were the responsibility of mothers who had failed to uphold their household appropriately.[35]

Print sources go beyond these abstractions in accounts that give shape to mothers who failed to prevent a prostitute's descent. Often, a mother's shortcoming was her indulgence. Jane B., as reported by the *Advocate,* grew up under the care of a mother whose unwillingness to administer discipline towards her only daughter left the girl recalcitrant and slovenly. Years later, after a life of disregard for domestic duties and proper behavior, Jane could be found "sitting on the steps of a dwelling, thinly clad…her whole appearance [exhibiting] the extreme of wretchedness." Having never been provided the moral or religious education that a girl requires from her mother, Jane led a debauched life of homelessness and alcoholism. Moreover, a childhood acquaintance found that "TOTAL DEPRAVITY was inscribed on every feature" of Jane's face—the corruption that came from her life as a prostitute had literally been marked upon her and became part of her appearance. This terrible fate, the account concludes, could have been avoided if Jane's mother had taken seriously the charge that God assigned her as the moral guide of her child.[36]

Lack of presence in a daughter's life was the other major way in which a mother could doom a girl to a life of prostitution. A family with too many children, a column in the *National Police Gazette* contended, was sure to have at least one girl go wayward—her mother's attention was too divided to instruct

---

35 "Improprieties in Dress," The Advocate of Moral Reform, July 15, 1836.

36 Capitalization is from the original document. "Fatal Effects of Indolence; or the Story of Jane B.—." The Advocate of Moral Reform, November 15, 1836.

her properly.[37] A mother's death, too, could lead her daughter to the brothel. Midcentury biographers of Helen Jewett, the famously murdered prostitute, observed with regret the fact that Jewett's mother had died when her daughter was a young girl. In particular, they noted that her mother's death made Helen vulnerable during puberty: "How deeply it is to be regretted that a girl…should not have had the watchful guardianship of a mother, at a time when the passions are bursting forth in their full strength."[38] Though she was dead, Jewett's mother was still placed at fault in these accounts for failing to impart on her daughter the care that might have prevented her from being seduced. A mother, therefore, must ensure that if death took her from her children before she had the chance to properly instruct them, she had an adequate substitute whom she could trust to provide guidance.

This responsibility then fell to the wider community of mothers. The *Advocate,* in particular, suggests that it was not sufficient for a mother to be content with maintaining proper morality in her own household; it was also incumbent upon her to help those children outside of her home who were in need. "Mothers especially ought to know, that while their beloved ones are safe beneath their watchful eye, the children of others, are reduced to a bondage most hopeless and degrading—and this…at our own doors." [39] This account and others like it sought to convince women that it was their duty to knock down doors in search of children living in depravity, just as moral reformers did. More importantly, however, these accounts put blame on even those mothers who had taught their children proper morality—so long as prostitution existed, it was a mother's charge to eradicate it.

The implication of this blame was a daunting one, for it meant that mothers were collectively responsible for an institution that existed on a far greater scale than they could address individually. Though a mother might have done all she could to prevent her daughter's ruin, the failure of the community of mothers

---

37 "National Police Gazette" column, National Police Gazette, October 31, 1846.

38 Authentic Biography of the Late Helen Jewett, a Girl of the Town, by a Gentleman Fully Acquainted with Her History (New York), 3-5 via Cohen, The Murder of Helen Jewett, 90.

39 "Extracts from Report of the Visiting Committee," Advocate of Moral Reform, July 1, 1837.

as a whole allowed prostitution to continue. Girls without mothers to protect and guide them were still in danger. Alone and without family, they might be lured into the comfort and love they were offered by another maternal figure—the brothel madam.

Madams

Having indulged in reading fiction, been improperly taught by their mothers, or brought to ruin at the hand of a seducer, girls in prostitution narratives invariably come to face the consequences of their sexual impropriety. Abandoned by their lovers and unable to return to their families, girls find they have nowhere to go but to a brothel.

If not by the man who seduced her, it is through a girl's peers that she makes initial contact with a brothel madam. Both the *National Police Gazette* and the *Advocate* report accounts in which sisters lead one another to a brothel. In some cases, this is done for malevolent purposes—girls might find it humorous to bring their younger sisters to a place of such depravity—while in others, it is done charitably—for instance, when a girl follows her sister willingly, feeling she has nowhere else to go.[40]

Whether a girl is brought by force or willingly, a madam greets her with warmth and compassion. "You are in the house of a friend," madam Mrs. Bishop tells young Lucy Pembroke in *The Gay Girls of New-York* using "the most honeyed accents."[41] Madams convince prostitutes to see their arrival at the brothel as a mere transition from one home to another, a brick, urban row house replacing a rural farmstead as the girls' home. With this new home comes a new mother to care for them. "Just make yourself easy, my lady, that's my advice," Madame S. tells her new boarder, Isabella, in Ned Buntline's *The Mysteries and Miseries of New York*. "Now be a good girl and I'll be a mother to you!"[42] Just as a Republican Mother

---

40 For a case in which a girl led her younger sister to a brothel because she found it humorous, see: "Restored," National Police Gazette, August 22, 1846. For a case in which girls willingly followed sisters to a brothel, see: "Missionary Intelligence," The Advocate of Moral Reform, July 15, 1836.

41 Thompson, The Gay Girls of New-York, 17.

42 Ned Buntline, The Mysteries and Miseries of New York: A Story of Real Life (New York: Berford & Co., 1848), 9.

occupies the heart of her home, a madam exists at the center of her brothel; she presents herself to her girls as being as responsible for their care, guidance, and instruction as a mother would be in any other home.

While characters within prostitution narratives might be lulled into complacency, if not entirely fooled, by the maternal persona adopted by madams, readers most certainly were not. A madam's duplicity and untrustworthiness would be obvious to antebellum readers from her first interaction with a newly arrived girl. "Anything you want to eat or drink shall be sent up," Madame S. tells Isabella at their first meeting, assuring the girl "you shall have books, or the papers, or anything that's reasonable!"[43] What a madam presents as offerings would be considered temptations by readers—fiction, after all, was what was believed to lead a girl into a life of prostitution in the first place, and gluttony and intemperance would only further her moral corruption. Providing these sources of sin to girls was not the care that mothers were meant to offer their daughters; madams were not teaching their girls piety or restraint, but rather giving them opportunities to indulge in the behaviors that destroyed their virtue.

As narratives continue, it becomes increasingly obvious to readers that a madam's purported maternal instincts are merely a guise used to exploit and profit from girls. Madams speak frankly about their intentions for fallen women, confessing that those in their care "will become a mine of gold to me," and celebrating how "these innocent looking girls always take the best, and command plenty of [profit]." [44] Because madams make these comments in private, only readers—not prostitutes in the story—are privy to these women's duplicity. This allows a madam to continue using her role as mother to her advantage, exploiting the trust a prostitute places in her in order to further ensnare the girl in the brothel. In *The Mysteries and Miseries of New York*, when Madame S. discovers Isabella's friends are searching for her in order to save the girl from Madame S.'s brothel, she doesn't force the girl into hiding. Instead, she acts sweetly towards Isabella, bringing the girl breakfast and complying with her request for lemonade

43 Buntline, The Mysteries and Miseries of New York, 8.

44 Thompson, The Gay Girls of New-York, 16-17.

rather than coffee. Her guard lowered by Madame S.'s show of benevolence, Isabella fails to realize that her drink is laced with a drug to put her to sleep, and is nowhere to be found once her friends come knocking at Madame S.'s door.[45]

It is only once a girl is firmly in a madam's grasp that the villainous woman reveals her true nature. Beneath a madam's "'painted old face,'" lies a woman capable of becoming "enraged...with fury in her looks" when at risk of losing one of her workers.[46] In *The Gay Girls of New-York,* Mrs. Bishop's determination to keep her prostitutes in order is put on display when she brawls with Hannah Sherwood, the aforementioned, good-natured if troublesome, prostitute who challenges the madam's authority. In shedding her motherly demeanor, Bishop makes clear to her prostitutes that she will not tolerate any behavior that might threaten her business. She banishes Hannah, and later takes vengeance on the girl by throwing a vial of vitriol on her face, blinding and severely disfiguring her former charge.[47]

This portrayed ability to shift between overt kindness and genuine ruthlessness made madams highly capable businesswomen in the minds of readers. Ideas that madams were prosperous and successful in their business were exacerbated by popular publications that claimed to offer inside information on the workings of brothels. "To Lovers of Horizontal Refreshments," a broadside that appeared in a Philadelphia publication, was purportedly written and signed by eight local madams. "At a meeting of old Bawds," the piece began, "the expected arrival from New York...of a large batch of handsome young whores, who are coming to this city with the evident intention of destroying our legitimate trade of fucking" was discussed. Dismayed by their new competition, the group of madams allegedly proclaimed "a crisis has occurred in our business that loudly calls for prompt and energetic action on our part to save us from disgrace and starvation."[48]

Prostitution is presented in this piece as a complex, proto-unionized business practice that involves cooperation between competing brothels in order

---

45 Buntline, The Mysteries and Miseries of New-York, 42-43.

46 Thompson, The Gay Girls of New-York, 20.

47 Thompson, The Gay Girls of New-York, 17-22, 74-75.

48 "To Lovers of Horizontal Refreshments," broadside, 1857, Box 1, John H. Hunt Papers 1849-1860, William L. Clements Library, Ann Arbor, Michigan.

to combat outside competition. Moreover, its existence suggests that prostitution is tolerated enough by society for such a document to be placed in print. The extreme vulgarity of this broadside, along with its unrealistic descriptions of women's bodies and genitalia, suggests that it was a satirical piece written by and intended for men involved in sporting culture.[49] To readers who came across this piece without realizing its authors and intended audience, however, the satire used here would be easy to miss.

During the antebellum era, humbug pieces appeared alongside real news stories, making the distinction between fact and fiction a blurry one for most readers. Editors were reluctant to inform readers of whether or not the fantastic stories they told audiences were true; instead, as Benjamin Day, editor of the New York *Sun,* stated when asked if a telescope he had written about was actually capable of discerning the moon's flora and fauna, "let every reader of the account examine it, and enjoy his own opinion."[50] In the case of "To Lovers of Horizontal Refreshments," readers were the ones with the power to determine whether or not this was an accurate portrayal of prostitution in Philadelphia. Anyone who read the piece and saw it as truth, rather than satire, would assume that madams did in fact work together, and that their business practices were deft and aggressive.

The business savvy ascribed to madams would be quite disturbing to audiences, for two primary reasons. First, it disrupts the ideal of women occupying the domestic sphere, while men work and earn wages. A madam does not conform to these norms. Though she might have a paramour, she is economically self-sufficient—her work might be even more lucrative than his. Madams, therefore, were subjects of social scrutiny because their business practice breached the domestic sphere women watching over young girls were meant to occupy. Second, and perhaps more importantly, a madam's success in her business ventures was based entirely on the sexual ruin of others. If these women truly were profiting, as popular narratives often depict, then numerous young girls must be

49 For more information on the Flash Press, a subgenre of antebellum urban journalism created and consumed by sporting men, see: Cohen, Gilfoyle, and Horowitz, The Flash Press: Sporting Male Weeklies in 1840s New York, Historical Studies of Urban America (Chicago: University of Chicago Press, 2008)

50 Tucher, Froth & Scum, 51-52.

working for them, and even more men must be coming to brothels to purchase their offerings. Not only was a madam stepping out of her role by running a business, then, but also she was doing so by luring others to ruin.

As older women living outside of respectable society and engaging in immoral behavior, madams were an obvious group for the authors of print sources to target as being responsible for the continued existence of prostitution. Unlike other characters in prostitution narratives, madams receive the sympathy of no writer. Their subversion of the tenets of motherhood for their own profit, at the expense of young girls, added to the repulsion that the public was likely to already feel because of their sexual immorality. Madams went further than mothers in causing a girl's ruin, for they actively manipulated the trust invested in them for selfish gain. To a public hoping to make sense of prostitution and why it existed, the presence of such crafty and treacherous women in society was horrifying; it might shake their faith in those around them, and compel them to reassess whom they could trust.

The Public

Print accounts chronicling the proliferation of prostitution in the antebellum era encouraged anxieties in Americans about the state of their society. Particular members of the public, to whose real world counterparts readers might have previously paid little attention, take on roles in these stories that center around a brothel and its inhabitants. Through these characters, authors put society as a whole on trial for the continued existence of prostitution, calling readers to be cautious of all those around them.

The wariness that these accounts recommended compounded the public's existing anxieties during the antebellum period. During this time, there was immense concern in parlor society about the plasticity of children's minds, and the ways in which exposure to sexual culture could affect development. Parents feared that a child who came across anything related to the era's growing dialogue around sex—including the print sources that discussed prostitution—would be encouraged into deviancy and sexual sin.[51] This meant that even those who aimed to actively fight against prostitution, like the moral reformers who used the rhetoric of motherhood in aid of their cause, actually "create the evil they would remedy" by drawing attention to sin.[52] Though their goals were moral, reformers only furthered the opportunities for girls to become prostitutes and boys to become seducers. Readers, then, were made to feel that their trust was misplaced in even those whose intent was virtuous.

This would be even more concerning because of print's suggestion that other segments of the public intentionally sought to perpetuate prostitution and the dangers it posed to women's spiritual and physical wellbeing. Chief among the groups depicted as such were abortionists. By removing from sex the inherent risk of pregnancy, abortionists were represented in antebellum accounts as allowing seducers to act uninhabited, thus encouraging ruin. Perhaps because women were held to a higher standard of morality than men, female abortionists in particular were lambasted in print. Though men could be labeled "cruel and violent," women who performed abortions were described with more venomous language, regarded as "modern vampyrs [sic]...who thrive by butchery and blood." [53] Madams Costello and Restell, two of the most prominent abortionists in 1840s New York, were the targets of smear campaigns in the *National Police Gazette* contending that the deaths of numerous women—even those who were not pregnant and thus had no reason to go to an abortionist—were their responsibility.[54] By holding abortionists responsible for deaths with which they had no clear connection, these accounts made them appear a public scourge of which the general populace should remain mindful.

If readers are part of the greater antebellum public, however, where can they place themselves in these accounts? Surely they did not seek to identify themselves with either the reformers who do more harm than good in their fervor, or with individuals like abortionists who purposefully preserve prostitution—

51 Horowitz, Rereading Sex, 120-122.

52 Whip and Satirist of New-York and Brooklyn, May 28, 1842, via Cohen, Gilfoyle, and Horowitz, The Flash Press, 74-75.

53 "Acquittal of Dr. Shove," National Police Gazette, October 24, 1846; National Police Gazette, December 5, 1846.

54 "Where is Restell?—Was She Murdered?", National Police Gazette, November 7, 1846.

but where else could they find themselves in prostitution narratives? In order to allow readers the opportunity to absolve themselves of blame for prostitution, an identifiable, moral segment of the public exists in many narratives. Stories abound, for example, of the heroism that neighbors display when they report local bawdy houses to the authorities (doing so, of course, without raising the public kerfuffle that moral reformers would).[55] In another case, when a German girl screams for help when about to be raped in a brothel, it is passersby who save her from harm.[56] In these members of the public, readers find what they imagine themselves as being. They, after all, would do their part to put a stop to prostitution if given the opportunity—it's everyone else in society who wouldn't do so.

When Albert Tirrell was acquitted for Maria Bickford's murder in April 1846, the *National Police Gazette* unflinchingly declared its outrage about the verdict. Both shocking and repugnant, the newspaper argued, was the escape of yet another seducer, who could continue his treachery throughout America.

Yet Tirrell is not the only player blamed in the *Gazette* for Bickford's death. According to the newspaper, Bickford had become dissatisfied with her life as a married woman in rural Maine when a group of female friends brought her to Boston for a short vacation. There, Bickford was "delighted by everything she saw—completely captivated—and on her return home…became dissatisfied with her humble condition." She became "passionately fond of dressing extravagantly," and she began to dream of a life in Boston that offered the excitement her current situation lacked.[57]

This infatuation with the glamor and opulence of the city was what made Bickford liable to be seduced by Tirrell. Had her friends not brought her to Boston, Bickford never would have fallen prey to the dangerous fantasies that tempted her away from the life of virtue she was leading in Maine. The *Gazette* even made note

55 "Trial for keeping a Disorderly House," National Police Gazette, March 20, 1847.
56 "Attempt to Commit a Rape," National Police Gazette, January 9, 1847.
57 "A Brief Sketch of the Life of Mary A. Bickford," National Police Gazette, December 6, 1845.

of how encouraging a woman's recklessness—as these friends did—could cause her to end up on the doorstep of a brothel.[58] Blame for Bickford's death, then, could be assigned to the members of her sex who had prodded her along the path leading to depravity. This didn't remove guilt from Tirrell, at least in the opinion of the *Gazette*—but it did mean that blame could be shared among multiple parties for a woman's fall.

Blame, as it manifests in prostitution narratives of the antebellum period, is not something that can be neatly assigned to a single actor; instead, it is shared by a variety of individuals in a single story. Such a wide range of characters, from mothers to madams to reformers to abortionists, would not exist in a prostitution narrative if blame could be neatly assigned to either the seduced or the seducer. The pattern of blame observed in Maria Bickford's story—of men being able to bring about a girl's ruin only because she or members of her sex have put her in compromising positions—is the most common one seen in antebellum narratives, yet others exist as well. No character is free of guilt in the body of prostitution narratives, and they all play a part in a girl's ruin.

Blame was a malleable feature of a fixed narrative that authors could use to assign fault to social groups that challenged their own values. It moved from account to account in accordance with a writer's worldview, shifting an unflattering spotlight on those people and behaviors that authors deemed deserving of social scrutiny. Moreover, the power of print in the antebellum era—Americans were reading more than ever before, as evidenced by circulation figures in the tens of thousands for publications like the *National Police Gazette* and the *Advocate of Moral Reform*—meant that this blaming had real consequences; Americans formed opinions about who was at fault for prostitution from what they read.[59] These stories shaped popular imagination, and enabled readers to ostracize groups different than them. They reflected and reinforced the prejudices of American society, and allowed readers an opportunity to evade responsibility for a societal evil.

---

58 "The Life of Maria Ann Bickford, the Murdered Adultress," National Police Gazette, December 6, 1845.

59 The Advocate claimed the largest audience of any evangelical periodical of the antebellum period, which some suggest was as high as 36,000. Lisa Shaver, "'Serpents,' 'Fiends,' and 'Libertines': Inscribing an Evangelical Rhetoric of Rage in the Advocate of Moral Reform," Rhetoric Review 30, no. 1 (December 17, 2010), 5; Rosenberg, "Beauty, the Beast, and the Militant Woman," 570; the Gazette's circulation exceeded 24,000 by 1847, its second year of publication, per figures reported in the paper itself.

In cases like Maria Bickford's, the American public had the opportunity to decide for itself who was at fault for a prostitute's death. The *Gazette's* account, like most other narratives of the antebellum era, offered apparent blame of one party and covert condemnation of another; it was therefore readers' decision as to whether Tirrell or Maria's female friends who excited her interest in a life of indulgence was at fault for her death. Readers likely disagreed on who was to blame for the "Boston Tragedy," but almost certainly found common ground in faulting the character whose behavior was more threatening to their worldview. In narratives that offered multiple groups as being responsible for prostitution, readers would subscribe to the interpretation that preserved their own sense of dignity; they would pick the story that kept blame for prostitution off of their shoulders.

WORKS CITED

Primary Sources

Newspapers and Periodicals:

Advocate of Moral Reform (New York), 1836-1840

National Police Gazette (New York), 1845-1847

New York Herald, 1842

Whip and Satirist of New-York and Brooklyn, 1842

Novels, Biographies, and Tracts:

Authentic Biography of the Late Helen Jewett, a Girl of the Town, by a Gentleman Fully Acquainted with Her History. New York.

Buntline, Ned. *The Mysteries and Miseries of New York: A Story of Real Life.* New York: Berford & Co., 1848.

Foster, George G. *New York by Gas-Light: With Here and There a Streak of Sunshine.* New York: Dewitt & Davenport, 1850.

Thompson, George. *The Gay Girls of New-York, Or, Life on Broadway Being a Mirror of the Fashions, Follies and Crimes of a Great City.* New York: 1853.

Bennett, John. *Strictures on Female Education, Chiefly as It Relates to the Culture of the Heart, in Four Essays.* Philadelphia, 1793.

Archival Documents:

"To Lovers of Horizontal Refreshments." Broadside. 1857. Box 1, John H. Hunt Papers 1849-1860, William L. Clements Library, Ann Arbor, Michigan.

Secondary Sources

Cohen, Patricia Cline. *The Murder of Helen Jewett: The Life and Death of a Prostitute in Nineteenth-Century New York.* Life and Death of a Prostitute in 19th Century New York, New York: Vintage Books, 1999.

Cohen, Patricia Cline, Timothy J. Gilfoyle, Helen Lefkowitz Horowitz. *The Flash Press: Sporting Male Weeklies in 1840s New York*. Historical Studies of Urban America. Chicago: University of Chicago Press, 2008.

Gilfoyle, Timothy J. *City of Eros: New York City, Prostitution, and the Commercialization of Sex, 1790-1920*. New York: Norton, 1992.

Hamilton, Gillian. "The Decline of Apprenticeship in North America: Evidence from Montreal." *The Journal of Economic History* 60, no. 3 (2000): 627–64.

Kelley, Mary "Genres of Print: Introduction." In *An Extensive Republic: Print, Culture, and Society in the New Nation, 1790-1840*. Edited by Robert A. Grossman and Mary Kelley (Chapel Hill: Published in association with the American Antiquarian Society by the University of North Carolina Press, 2010).

Kelly, Catherine E. *In the New England Fashion: Reshaping Women's Lives in the Nineteenth Century*. Ithaca, N.Y.: Cornell University Press, 1999.

Meckel, Richard A. "Educating a Ministry of Mothers: Evangelical Maternal Associations, 1815-1860." *Journal of the Early Republic* 2, no. 4 (1982): 403–23.

Rosenberg, Carroll Smith. "Beauty, the Beast and the Militant Woman: A Case Study in Sex Roles and Social Stress in Jacksonian America." *American Quarterly* 23, no. 4 (1971): 562–84.

Shaver, Lisa. "'Serpents,' 'Fiends,' and 'Libertines': Inscribing an Evangelical Rhetoric of Rage in the Advocate of Moral Reform." *Rhetoric Review* 30, no. 1 (December 17, 2010): 1–18.

Tucher, Andie. *Froth & Scum: Truth, Beauty, Goodness, and the Ax Murder in America's First Mass Medium*. Chapel Hill: University of North Carolina Press, 1994.

Winning Essays
Granader Prize for Excellence in Upper-Level Writing (humanities)

10 Months In Europe

Courtney Cook

From English 325 / Art of the Essay

Nominated by Jaimien Delp

This essay demonstrates a young writer doing the hard, honest work that surrounds such a complex and personal genre. At the heart of each carefully crafted scene and each attentive, perceptive detail is a longing for answers to questions that are at once captivating, inspired, and human. This is a writer tapping into the abstractions and vague notions that so often take residence in our memories of events, and demanding tangible, realized understanding. Her questions – How is it that one can recall such painful, even traumatic periods of one's life with fondness, even longing? How might a landscape, or a community, heal us? What does it mean to be broken, and what does it mean to be whole? What is happiness? – inspire a process of sifting and reflecting that invites the reader into a portrait so vivid and honest, they can't help but find connection here. The work shifts seamlessly from scene and reflection to meaning, landing on powerful insights that reach well beyond the world of La Europa Academy, the setting for Courtney's essay.

Jaimien Delp

10 Months in Europe

Before La Europa Academy was a residential treatment center for at risk teenage girls, it was a bed and breakfast, mainly serving newlyweds. Located in Murray, Utah, a suburb smack in the middle of Park City and Salt Lake City, La Europa offered convenience and a hint of extravagance. As couples pulled up to the tan mansion they were greeted by two large lion statues at each side of the front door, which opened to reveal an entryway with a four-tiered, trickling fountain. Each room in La Europa was named after a country in Europe: Munich, Brussels, Helsinki, Barcelona, Budapest. The honeymooners could then say they spent their week in Dublin and they wouldn't necessarily be lying, like a secret only the two of them knew. The backyard had a stone patio, and a pond full of hungry koi fish ready to be fed. There was a tennis court to take lessons on and a large pool to swim in when it was summer. Surrounded by towering mountains and blue skies two hundred and thirty days a year (the others were spent with snow filled clouds that turned Utah into a scene out of a snow globe), La Europa was hardly short of a dream.

That is, for those who stayed in it when it was a bed and breakfast. When I arrived at La Europa at the age of thirteen, it had been converted into a residential treatment center three years prior. The pool had been drained, gradually having been filled in with dirt and rainwater. The tennis court was cracked, the fountain in the entryway had long been dry, and the pond in the backyard had more browned leaves in it than fish. One thing remained the same, and that was the room names. I moved into Brussels, and joked with the other girls about telling everyone back home that we'd spent the year traveling Europe once we were released. We had that joke in common with the honeymooners.

It was hard for me to picture La Europa as it had been in its prime; what it would have been like to have the house filled with happy couples instead of depressed and struggling teenage girls. Even though none of the couches in the great room matched, and the carpets were stained, and the heat didn't work in

Munich or the addition we had nightly meetings in, and all that had once made La Europa beautiful had been tarnished, it was still beautiful to us in a way that only home can be. We often mistook that beauty for hatred the way that one often does when thinking about home, because it's easy to hate something you know will always love you back. It's like fighting with your mom: you know you can say the most hurtful thing in the entire world to her and she'll still love you endlessly, and despite your words, know you love her the same. Sometimes I talk to the other girls I was in treatment with, and we all agree that La Europa was the best worst time of our lives.

Though we were at a treatment center, we were also living with our best friends, and the ceilings were high so when we laughed the sound floated through the whole house, and someone was always laughing. The same went for crying, but I remember the laughing more. Guitars lined the walls of the great room and sat in cases under our beds, some of us with voices so lovely that the world seemed to fall silent every time they opened their mouths to sing while they played. Every night someone would ask Sasha or Becky or Kayla to sing, and we'd all gather round in awe. Sometimes another girl would play for us, and even though they weren't as good, we would listen all the same.

La Europa's program was based in art therapy, so it seemed every wall was covered in art. Next to the bulletin board that had our weekly schedule and stated which therapy groups took place on what day, there were paintings and printed photographs and drawings we'd made. Most of the paintings were done on cardboard because we were short on money and didn't have canvas, with little images of bananas or a brand logo showing through the paint if you looked at them in a certain light. Even our teachers were artists; the walls in the entranceway were lined with portraits of girls who had completed the program that our art teacher, Jill, had lovingly drawn for them as graduation gifts. Looking at them was like some kind of hope: yes, you were in a treatment center. Yes, you were likely going to be there for a year. Yes, it would be hard. But also: yes, you'd make it out of there, and like those girls on the wall, you'd be happy.

I spent the days before I was admitted to La Europa with my parents in a house we rented in the mountains of Park City. We watched movies and my dad made me crepes that weren't cooked all the way through and were fat like pancakes from the altitude. My mom wrote me a song, recorded it on GarageBand, and sheepishly handed it to me on a CD to listen to when I missed her. Knowing I would be apart from them for the first time ever, we soaked up our time together by eating our way through Park City's restaurants and exploring the small street fairs that lined the hilly roads. When the time had finally come for me to check in, we made the forty-five minute drive through the winding canyons to Murray. When we were five minutes away my mom turned around from the front seat.

"Don't judge it on the first few days, Court. They follow you around for awhile, but it'll get better. You'll love it." Her voice was warm.

"I know," I said. I hadn't, but I knew it was too late to turn back.

After I had been stripped searched, had all my belongings checked in, and said goodbye to my parents, I understood what my mom was talking about in the car. I was told that for the first week of my stay I'd be on what was called 'Safety'. On Safety you're required to be within five feet of a staff at all times. You have to eat one hundred percent of your food, wait thirty minutes to go to the bathroom after meals, and every time you use the bathroom you have to count while you go. While you shower a staff has to sit outside the glass door and watch the drain. You're not allowed to wear shoes, and when the other girls leave campus for rec night, dinner, or to go to the rec center to work out, you have to stay. I was told that if after a week I hadn't hurt myself I'd be moved off of Safety to level 1 of the program, and then I'd be allowed to start showering alone, wearing shoes, and going off campus. I'd still have to be in a staff's line-of-sight at all times, though, and would still have to count in the bathroom. Eventually, I'd work my way to level 6, gaining privileges as I went, and then I'd be able to graduate and go home.

It was summer, and though I was on Safety and following all of its many rules, it took me a week to fully comprehend the new space I was in. It seemed everything was at La Europa the way it was everywhere else. There were friend groups and the worry of where to sit at meals. Girls played Mario Kart during free time and took guitar and dance lessons on Sundays. Summer school was a breeze and my first day in science class we made Baked Alaska as a way to learn about some property of chemistry I've long forgotten, though we cooked it in the same oven we were cooking chicken in for lunch and it tasted much more like chicken than it did a sweet dessert. In math class we watched episodes of CSI and discussed the mathematical principles they mentioned while they were solving crimes. Though we were all admitted to La Europa because we were a suffering from immense depression and often trauma, and all the ways trauma and depression manifests, it seemed everyone was, for the most part, happy. There was a lot of smiling and laughter in a way you wouldn't anticipate at a treatment center. Aside from the two hours a day we spent in group therapy, the three hours a week we spent in individual therapy, and our nightly 'Community' sessions where we spoke about our goals and what we were struggling with, we were almost normal.

Renée showed up a week into what would become my ten-month stay. She looked down a lot and was shy in a way that was almost painful, with a voice she made purposely a few octaves higher than it was naturally so she sounded like a child. When Renée moved into Brussels with my roommate Lily and I, we were happy to have someone so sweet living with us. Our happiness turned to horror and annoyance, however, after we spent a few nights with her.

At night, whatever had brought Renée to La Europa came out with a vengeance. She kicked and screamed in her sleep, thrashing beneath her royal purple duvet cover. The night staff that monitored us in our sleep and came in every fifteen minutes with a flashlight to see if we all were still where we should be would wake her, and she'd have a few minutes of peace before succumbing to her night terrors again. Each morning the staff would take her to the laundry room and she'd wash her sheets without any explanation. For the first few days Lily and I didn't understand, until our room began to reek of urine and a staff set up two fans to constantly try to air out the smell because the windows were permanently locked.

It's custom that when you arrive at La Europa you tell what brought you there at your first night's Community meeting. Renée refused to talk for her first three nights, but on the fourth night she finally spoke up. She told us she'd been raped daily by her father, brother, and uncles since she was seven, and that when she was placed in foster care she began to be abused again. She bounced from foster home to foster home until she finally found a loving family that adopted her and sent her to La Europa to process what had been done to her and heal. None of us knew what to say; I think Renée's trauma was too deep for any of us to process. So we looked down and picked at our cuticles and thanked her for sharing, because it was all we could think to do. As soon as she spoke, I felt so badly for being upset about the smell that permeated our room. I was glad I hadn't asked her why she was washing her sheets.

Everything at La Europa was routine. On weekdays we'd wake at 6:15 for gym class and on weekends there was no gym so we were allowed to sleep until 10. On Mondays and Wednesdays we went to the rec center for gym, the other days we either did yoga in the dance room in our schoolhouse or P90x in the great room. We each took four classes that alternated on a block schedule Monday through Thursday from 8:30 until 11:30, then came lunch. Wednesday was breakfast for lunch, and Monday was dessert night. We were allowed to shave on Wednesdays and Sundays, supervised by a staff, and only with an electric razor. Every third Friday we went to the Salt Lake City public library, which had four stories and huge glass elevators some girls, including me, were too afraid to ride. The other Fridays we spent volunteering at the soup kitchen or the animal shelter. After lunch we'd have an elective class, then group therapy, then dinner, free time, study hall, Community, and then we'd sleep. The staff called getting ready for bed "hygiene" and it was scheduled into our day.

On Friday nights one girl would be allowed to choose where we'd go out to dinner, and her answer was always Chipotle, no matter who was asked. The staff at Chipotle knew all of our names and orders by heart and knew to expect us at 6:30 sharp every Friday night. On Saturdays we had movie night where one girl would be allowed to choose an approved movie that was PG-13 or under, and we'd all gather around and watch on an old TV that we'd push around on a metal stand on wheels. Then Sunday morning we'd wake up and deep clean our house for three hours or as long as it took us, do homework, have pizza for dinner, then some girls would go to Alcoholics Anonymous while some of us had a two hour period called "reflection" where we were only allowed to journal or sit silently in our beds or read, and then we'd have hygiene, and go to sleep.

Because everything was so routine, tiny things meant the world to us. Something as small as calling 'shotty' before a car ride was riveting. Sitting in the front seat of what we called the "treatment vans," the huge white vans with tinted black windows that seated fourteen and transported us everywhere, was a huge privilege. This was not only because you had to be above level three in order to do so, but because you got to choose the music for the entirety of the ride.

Getting shotty for the ride to the rec center on Monday and Wednesday mornings didn't mean much—the ride was less than ten minutes. But on the nights we drove to the canyons to roast pink starburst and marshmallows over a fire while we held Community, or to the Jamba Juice and Nickel Cade, and the ride was twenty minutes or more, sitting shotty was heaven. Though every CD we burned on our home passes to bring back for the car rides had to be approved by the staff song by song, and our radio choices could be vetoed at any moment if they so much as swore, in a residential treatment center where everything we did was monitored the freedom to choose music in the car was as close to true freedom as we could get.

The Nickel Cade was a cheesy arcade filled with Skee Ball, Whack-A-Mole, and every other arcade game one could think of, and every game cost only a nickel. We weren't allowed to play with the games that had guns, but other than that the Nickel Cade was ours to conquer. For girls who lived in a treatment center without access to cell phones, iPods, or even the Internet, a game of pinball felt like magic.

We were each allotted five dollars in nickels, handed to us in red solo cups, that we could use for whatever we wanted from the tickets we earned. There was no saving your nickels for the next rec night, or for your next fun pass with your mentor; no one was allowed to have money at La Europa. To do so would be a flight risk, which staff spent immeasurable time trying to prevent, so much so that every piece of clothing we had was inventoried and we were only allowed a select number of clothing in each category. In the morning when we got dressed the staff in charge of us that day would mark what we were wearing down in our chart. That way, if we ran away they'd know what to tell the police: "She was wearing that blue shirt with red stripes and black skinny jeans from Urban Outfitters. Green socks from Costco, gray Uggs with the fur turned down. A black zip up sweatshirt, unzipped, Officer."

After we spent an hour toying with joy sticks, playing air hockey, and trying to hit the jackpot on every game we played, we'd gather around the glass countertop of the prize area holding onto our receipt from the ticket counter and survey what we could afford. Most of us would walk out with a keychain even though we weren't allowed to own bags to hang them on because of the flight risk, or a handful of Laffy Taffy and a Tootsie Roll. It didn't matter that the prizes were lame, it just felt good to get outside the walls of La Europa, for awhile.

We'd load into the treatment vans and drive home, piling out of the cars and line up by the door, ready to be checked in. Forming three lines in the entryway next to the fountain, we'd wait to be patted down by one of the staff. The illusion of normalcy we'd had while we were out would be shattered as a staff would run her hands down the sides of both our legs, feel their way around the waist of our pants, under our bra straps and band, under our arms and in our pockets. We'd have to shake out our ponytails, shake out our shoes, take off our socks, and then do a mouth check. Using our fingers to pull apart our cheeks, we'd move our tongues every possible way to prove we weren't hiding anything, and then cough, hard. They had to make sure we weren't hoarding our nickels, as if nickels could've gotten us anywhere. We all knew we were trapped, whether we liked it or not, at 1220 Vine St in Murray, Utah, until we graduated or our insurance ran out and our parents couldn't pay the 10,000 dollar a month price tag to help us get better anymore.

Usually at least one girl out of our group of thirty-two would have a break down each day, and at any given moment in time at La Europa you could almost guarantee that someone in the house was crying. Group therapy was usually hard and some girl would speak and unintentionally trigger another. There were often days that marked a year since a girl was raped or when she had to have an abortion or the one month mark of being sober for a girl addicted to meth who yearned for it all of the time. But some days, there was a lull in the sadness in the house. Every girl who applied to level up would have her request granted by the Treatment Team, no one would cry in group therapy, home passes would be approved. Community lasted only a few minutes while everyone spoke about how they were doing well.

If your therapist felt the good energy in the house they might be extra nice to you and take you to Stop-N-Shop to get you a candy bar or soda before therapy, or let you have therapy in a park somewhere if it was sunny out. Sometimes the staff would feel stir crazy and let us walk down the road to Wheeler Farm and pet the pigs and horses and shoo flies off of the cows and take pictures in the hay. Or if the budget had been increased recently, we'd be allowed extra treats on rec night and walk to Woody's, a drive in diner down the street, to pick up grasshopper milkshakes. During those days, I wondered if we were as damaged as we seemed, or if we'd just had a lot of bad days that were strung together in a long row and we were finally out of the woods.

Other days, everything went wrong and if one person started crying everyone would start to cry with them. Some days we were ushered to our rooms quickly and without explanation, told that we were to stay in our beds and read or journal and be absolutely silent until further notice.

The first time this happened to me I remember how Rachel's screams could be heard from every room in the house. Our great room had two story ceilings, and the second floor was connected by a walkway that looked over both it and the kitchen. Rachel was crumpled on one of the green suede couches, her body heaving with sobs. Four staff surrounded her, ready to put her in a hold if necessary. Until Rachel's situation was fixed, or she was taken to a hospital to be sedated, we all were to remain in our beds. None of us knew what Rachel had done to become so upset, but we knew what had brought her here. We all had a story; Rachel's was that she'd taken a nail and hammered it into her leg down to the bone. The hole never truly healed and was always leaking, like a faucet that never fully shut off.

It seemed most the staff had just as little information about what was going on as we did. As we sat in our beds, fidgeting with both anxiety and boredom, they texted on their Nokia staff phones with impressive speed. I always wondered what they were saying, but that day I did so more than usual. After two hours of mindless journaling and wishing I'd checked out another book at the library when we'd gone two weeks before, the staff watching us, Devon, stood up.

"When we were doing room checks today a staff found Rachel's eyeliner sharpener in the sharps closet with a blade missing. We've found it in a vent in her room. We can have dinner now."

And like that, it was over. Rachel was escorted to her room accompanied by two staff. For the next twenty-four hours she'd sit in her bed on Shutdown, the level of our program below even Safety. Shutdown was La Europa hell.

As Rachel went up to her room the rest of us went downstairs for dinner. We gathered at our giant table and ate the horrible fried tofu our chef, Carrie, had made. We laughed and joked and told stories too loudly, happy to be able to talk again. Even though we were in treatment, even though we all suffered from depression and anxiety and so many of us had been raped and some of us had tried to kill ourselves and most of us cut ourselves when we were sad, we were happy. At least for that moment, at least everyone was but Rachel. And hopefully one day, that happiness would last forever.

La Europa went from housing newlyweds and vacationing couples who wanted get away and relax to housing thirty-two broken teenage girls. The girls were always replacing one another; as one girl would graduate, another would be admitted. The girls I met when I was admitted to La Europa with were not the girls who were there when I left, and the personality of the house morphed to accommodate whoever was there at the time. That house was always changing, but seemed to hold onto those who had been there before. The air in La Europa felt different than it did elsewhere, aged in a way. Like it knew something that we'd have to stay there to learn.

I often wonder what it would have been like to have gone to La Europa when it wasn't a treatment center, but it seems too painful to picture. I don't want to imagine the fence in the backyard stripped of all of the handprints of the girls who have graduated and wanted to leave their mark on the place that fixed them. I don't want to imagine a time where that giant tan house was perceived as happier than it was when I was there, because I didn't, and still don't, believe there is a possibility of a place more beautiful.

La Europa, the rec center, our schoolhouse, Woody's, Wheeler Farm, the canyons, Chipotle, the Nickel Cade, and Murray, Utah as a whole nursed us back to life. They showed us goodness when none of us saw good. They knew we were broken and instead of fearing or judging us, they helped put us back together through time and open hearts and strict rules and Sunday night pizza and a waterless fountain and grasshopper milkshakes.

I like to believe our house at 1220 Vine Street was happy to have made this transformation from bed and breakfast to treatment center, that it somehow felt proud to see all of us girl's transformations taking place within its walls. I like to believe that there was some sense of purpose in standing up tall and providing us with something comforting and constant in a time where we believed everything was changing or falling apart. That it felt proud to bear witness to our struggle. Originally it must've seemed like the love was leaving the place when it was changed from honeymooners paradise to a residential treatment center, but I swear I've never felt more love than from the thirty-two girls and dozens of staff who wanted me to not only live, but to be happy.

On Nights Like These

Claire Wood

From English 425 / Advanced Essay Writing
Nominated by John Rubadeau

One of the best essays I've received in forty-one years at the college level, the last thirty-one at Michigan. While the subject matter is perhaps a tad risqué, the writing is absolutely gorgeous—full of wonderful details to show excellent parallelism, superior and very mature diction, subtle use of leitmotiv, et cetera.

John Rubadeau

On Nights Like These

You stand on a balcony.

You always do, on nights like these.

It is dark — wonderfully dark — a darkness so thick and inky that if you reach out and cup your hands, the night puddles in your palms.

From your shoulders dangles a night shirt — this long, gray, beautifully baggy masterpiece that hangs low and tickles the tops of your knees. You wear no underwear. You relish the feeling — this nakedness, this nudity. A warm night wind flits beneath your shirt and licks your upper thigh, tenderly.

You look up at the moon, the stupid, white face staring down at you.

This is me, you say. Bare, stripped.

The moon says nothing.

You like it like this — just you and the moon. You are safe in its silence, in the lame, blank stare.

You finger a bottle of Merlot. Your lips slip over the mouth. The liquid is soft, sweet; you don't gag. It drifts across your tongue, pooling in your cheeks before dripping down your throat.

But then, for a moment, it isn't wine.

And you are back.

You wear black. You always do, for times like these. It is assumed. This is what he likes: the trimmed black panties — deliciously thin, scooping sensually over your hips; the ebony cups of the bra dipping low, so low, covering your nipples, but only just.

You are hot, fuckable.

He approves.

Your lips move down him easily. The action is practiced, methodical.

Give him anticipation, but only slightly.

Kiss the arm; trace the rib; hover at the abdomen—

Then lower.

Your tongue circles the head; your lips move over. Your mouth moves down the shaft.

A sigh from the pillowcase.

Down. Up. Down. Up.

You study the skin as you bob. The dark, tan, rippling musculature. You wonder how many push-ups, sit-ups, crunches, curls it takes to get skin like this.

And you hate it — this horribly beautiful skin.

You hate the way it looks, the way it feels, the way it smells. The way it twitches as your tongue flicks across the surface.

You are repulsed, disgusted.

Down. Up.

But the taste—

The taste is what you hate the most. You don't hate it; you despise it. You loathe it because it lingers. The smell, the sight, the feeling— those fade. They are swallowed up by inky night and washed away by icy showers.

But the taste—

The taste stays with you. The taste of a man lingers long after the man disappears. It clings to your tongue, your cheeks, the back of your throat. You will try to wash it away with moonlight and Merlot.

It won't.

In minutes, you hear it— the sad, choking-turtle sound. He is there. A breath, and liquid squirts into your mouth. All at once, then barely at all.

You suck softly. He groans; you swallow. He drips down your throat. You gag, but hide it.

You lie down next to him. He doesn't move: eyes closed, dick limp.

You stretch out sensually, running your big toe along the sheets. You know he won't touch you. You don't expect him to, anymore.

You take too long. The words echo in your mind.

The voice is impersonal, flat. He is busy. Women— they take too long. *It isn't you, my dear.* It's genetic. He has that thing— you remember? He told you. He is busy. It isn't personal. It isn't personal. We are in college; we are busy. He is busy.

He tells you again. *I'm a busy man.*

I know, you say. Feign a smile. *I understand.*

You are about to leave, now. You are dressed, standing in the doorway. He stands before you, one arm stretched up the wall, gazing down at you playfully, casually, condescendingly.

You let me stand you up again today, he says. *Why'd you do that?*

You shrug. He doesn't care that you were waiting for him. He never will. His eyes watch yours. You hate these, too — these majestic, insolent, beautiful gray-green eyes.

You know I love to blow you off, he teases. *Don't let me stand you up next time.* He smirks softly, extends a chiseled arm and flicks the tip of your nose with his index finger.

But now you are back, with the moonlight and the Merlot. You call your sister. Alice. Blonde, skinny, ruthless. You always do, on nights like these.

"I did it again," you say.

"What?" she asks.

"Him."

She is silent for a moment. Alice hates him; you know that. You hate him; she knows that. She doesn't understand.

"At least you get an orgasm out of it," Alice says. Alice is like that. Cold, hard, matter-of-fact. You say she's a realist; she says she's a bitch.

"Oh, no," you explain. "No orgasm."

"What do you mean, no orgasm?"

"I mean, he doesn't— *do me.*"

"What do you mean, he doesn't *do you?*" Alice is appalled.

"I take too long." You rationalize.

"How long do you take?"

You think. "Fifteen minutes. Maybe ten."

"I make my salad in fifteen minutes," Alice says.

"He doesn't eat salad," you say.

"So you just blow him?"

"Yeah." You swallow more wine. It is thick, soft, sticky.

She pauses, thinking.

"Do you like him?" she asks.

"No."

"Do you love him?"

"No."

You loved a man, once. You still do.

He is tall, with a crooked smile and blue eyes so sharp and soft that when you sink into them, they prick you, tenderly. He looks at you, and you forget, for a moment, what it is to breathe.

You won't tell him, though. About breathing, or forgetting to.

Alice has to go. She is meeting someone— a friend. The receiver clicks; she is gone.

You keep the phone pressed to your ear after she disappears, savoring the warm, electric hum against your cheek.

You lower the phone and raise the Merlot. It is half-empty, now, the bloody red inside sloshing, sloshing, sloshing. Your lips slip over the bottle, and, in a flash, you are back, standing in the doorway, gazing up into insolent, gray-green eyes.

He leans against the wall, arm stretched up, looking down at you. His words play in your mind, over and over and over like a bad record.

Why'd you let me stand you up? You know I love blowing you off. Don't let me blow you off this time. His words slip slimy and wet in your ear like a snake's tongue. The finger flicks playfully, casually, condescendingly against your nose.

You take too long. I'm a busy man.

You know I love blowing you off.

Flick.

Flick.

Flick.

You feel the tears welling up, the emptiness brimming inside you.

The gray-green eyes watch, amused. They flicker. They know you will come back. You know you will, too. Return, and fill that gap, that hollow. To him, you know, this is all you are: a wet tongue, an open mouth. He doesn't have to tell you to tell you. The eyes say it all.

Why'd you let me stand you up?

You know I love blowing you off.

It isn't personal. You take too long. I'm busy. I'm a busy man.

Your arm winds back, and your fist slams into his nose. You hear the crunch.

He yells, bends over. His blood is on your knuckles. You notice immediately — the jarring scarlet, dripping across your palms and pooling on the kitchen tile. And for a startling instant, you feel it—

Self.

The blood dripping from your palm is power. You don't need him.

And in that moment, you *are*.

But you won't do it. The action is too brazen, irrational: defenseless in its defense. If you hit him, you lose him. Bite back, and he will let you go.

You will be alone.

So you are back again, with the moonlight and the Merlot. Your lips slide over the bottle. The wine slips across your tongue, down your throat. You don't gag.

You think of the other one — the one you always think of, on nights like these.

You might tell him you are in love.

He would tell you he isn't.

I don't love you. I'll never love you. You hear his would-be words; they echo in your ears, make your chest ache.

He will never know you the way you want him to.

But if you tell him, at least, you will feel it. That feeling, in your breast. That gunshot. That blade, ripping through your skin, splitting your heart right down the middle so that the two ventricles quiver separately, connected only by one shuddering, blood-red string. *Thump-thump. Thump-thump.*

I don't love you. I'll never love you.

The blood spreads across your chest. It trickles down your breast, dripping in thick raindrops from your nipple.

Now, instead of nothingness, you feel pain.

Real pain.

He does not love you; he will never love you.

It is the stab caused by vulnerability and courage. Only love can hurt this bad.

But this— this, my dear, is what you are afraid of.

Isn't this what you fear?

That gunshot. That blade.

So don't tell him.

Make love to the man you don't love and who doesn't love you.

Stand on the balcony. Slip your lips over the mouth of the bottle; swallow. Let the inky black surround you, caress you, kiss you; let the tongue of the wind lick your untouched thigh. Shed a tear with the stars, and whisper to the moon—

oh, how beautiful it might be to be alive.